No Free Milk

The Proverbs 31 Woman
defined

Shea A. Cameron

Unless otherwise noted, all Scripture used is New International Version 1984.

Cover Design:

RedLife Creative

Stock Images on Cover:

Dreamstime.com

Business woman holding a sign
© Dean Mitchell

Black male hand on heart
© Les3photo8

Preacher 1
© Ken Hurst

Two men of different ethnicity
© Alexandre Miguel Da Silva Nunes

No Free Milk

ISBN 978-0-9852885-0-1

For more information, write to:

Agape Consulting Group, LLC.

Shea A. Cameron

1629 K Street, N.W.

Suite 300

Washington, DC 20006

www.nofreemilk.net

info@nofreemilk.net

Dedication

This book is dedicated to the most loving, most encouraging, most caring, most tender-hearted woman I have ever known. She was a prayer warrior, and a woman of great faith. I would often tell people, she was the first person I ever saw Jesus in; and not because she took me to church with her every Sunday (which she did,) but because of her love walk. Christ was exemplified in her not because of sheer religious acts... but because of the type of fruit her life produced.

This book is dedicated to Ann Hagans, my grandmother, who went home to be with the Lord in 1997. Her life and legacy has forever left an imprint on my heart, and she was my very best friend.

Thank you grandma for your example; and thank you for your genuine, unhindered love. I will always love and appreciate you, and all you've done for me. The impact you've had on my life, as well as the lives of many others, is an eternal one. Until we meet again...

Acknowledgments

My sincere thanks and appreciation to Jonathan Booth for his editorial expertise on this manuscript, to Vita Redding for creative design of the cover, to my son Jordan for pushing and encouraging me to finish; and to my friends and associates for their support and encouragement with this project.

Contents

Introduction

The life of the Christian woman is a story consisting of the intricate experiences of love, motherhood, and intimacy with her Lord. So often, as little girls, we view the story of our lives through the eyes of a princess, in hopes that our journey will resemble a beautiful fairytale; filled with adventure, safety, and romance. Although we all hope and seek for a happy ending, our journey doesn't necessarily begin that way. We all have had experiences that left us either feeling disappointed, broken, confused, or maybe even spiteful. As a result of our choices and interactions with others, we have found ourselves facing situations and circumstances that have enlightened us of our need for healing, deliverance, and direction. In the pages of NO FREE MILK, we find that there is a way that the Lord has made for us to find ourselves refocused, strengthened, and equipped; enabling us to find true love while avoiding what isn't. As life is filled with many lessons, we discover that the plan of God addresses our desires and provides a path to obtain them righteously and without compromise.

This book serves as a mirror and a light, both revealing the truth of our common detours and providing directed insight for our life journey.
NO FREE MILK asks us questions to determine if we are waiting in vain hope or preparing for the promise of purpose. We will also discover the essential
attributes necessary for successful relationships that are rewarding, yet pleasing to God.

As we turn the pages, refreshing wisdom unfolds that helps to gently brisk away the lingering condemning thoughts of past decisions, making room for a new beginning in wholeness. We will be lovingly guided by the relevant truth and application from the Word of God necessary for healthy relationships and acute thinking.

NO FREE MILK will teach and remind us that true love is derived and established from the Father in heaven, beginning with our personal relationship with Him, through His son, Jesus Christ. This book is about the joyous liberty that is discovered once we address every hindrance that prevents us from being spiritually and emotionally healthy as well as in our relationships, including marriage.

I thank you for embracing this purposeful encounter with destiny. Now is the appointed time to allow the truth of God's word to permeate our hearts and minds, refusing to settle for anything less than what is pure, holy, and truly satisfying. Declare with me, that from this point forward, there will be NO FREE MILK!

Waiting is Good... BUT are you waiting in the right, or wrong line???

After meeting a particular gentleman of interest, we hit it off great for the first couple of weeks. However, I could literally pinpoint the day that things began to shift. He stopped being as attentive, he called me less, and the little things he would do daily in the beginning, like ask me, "If I was still feeling him?", he stopped doing. I'm not really sure why this happened... but it did. We were never physically, or even virtually intimate; and because we met via the Internet, most of our communication was done by social networking, email, and phone.

As soon as I started to feel like I was beginning to lose his interest, I began to feel extremely melancholy as I had become accustomed to our daily conversations, encouraging and romantic emails, as well as the feeling of exclusivity that he had given me. However, just as quickly as I began to feel sad about losing what I believed to be a potential "keeper," these words came to me... "What if you're waiting in the wrong line?"

"Wait on the LORD: be of good courage, and he shall strengthen thine heart: wait, I say, on the LORD."

Psalm 27:14 (KJV)

So often, as believers we are told to, "Wait on the Lord... and be of good courage!" This is wonderful and true, as we should absolutely, "Wait on the Lord." However, do we really know what that means? There are many who are waiting for God to do something special in their lives... yet, they're waiting in vain.

WHICH WRONG LINES are you waiting in? Are you waiting for someone to love you that God never purposed for your life? Are you waiting for someone to make a decision about whether or not they will commit to a relationship, when God had nothing to do with putting you with that person in the first place? Are you waiting for an abusive situation to change when God has already released you from it? Are you waiting to be with a lover when God is waiting to restore your marriage? Are you waiting for that job promotion when you know God told you to start that business? The sooner you get out of the wrong line and into the right one... is the sooner you'll get to your destiny!

You could be one that's waiting on the Lord to bless an endeavor that consistently fails; yet you are unable to shift and transition to where God would have you to be for this season. It's hard enough as it is to wait; but to wait so long and FINALLY get to the check-out only to discover that you were in the "15-items-or-less" lane when you know there is absolutely nothing "express" about your destiny! Always remember that as a child of the Most High God, your steps are ordered; therefore, your destiny and journey of events EACH have an appointed time, and season. "The steps of a good man are ordered by the LORD: and he delights in his way." Psalm 37:23 (KJV)

Guard Your Heart

"**A**bove all else, guard your heart, for it is the well-spring of life." Proverbs 4:23

Guarding your heart is important for many reasons. First, it contains the very essence of who you are as an individual; and that information is proprietary as it does not belong to just anyone! Always know that the essence of who you are, the deep place of your being, should be well guarded; as everyone has not earned the right to be privy to that information. The deepest part of your personhood should not be open and public; but rather private with limited, restricted access only to those who need to know, deserve to know, or have earned the right to know the contents within!

Restricted Access

The sign on your heart should read "Restricted Access," as though you are guarding a treasure....

because you are! If you were a bank owner, would you let just anyone have access to your vault? Absolutely not! Sure, they're welcome to come into the lobby, but even then it must be during business hours! In addition, even the individuals behind the teller windows are screened before being hired for that position. However, only a "select few" have access to the bank vault! The vault is highly protected, guarded, and has restricted access; so much so, that the bank vault tellers must obtain special clearances before being hired for this position.

According to Wikipedia, a bank vault is a secure space where money, valuables, records, and documents can be stored. It is intended to protect its contents from theft, unauthorized use, fire, natural disasters, and other threats; just like a safe. But unlike safes, vaults are an integral part of the building within which they are built, using armored walls and a tightly fashioned door closed with a complex lock. For example, Fort Knox is noted as one of the most impenetrable bank vaults in the world, and protected by a 22-ton vault door, because of the value of its treasure inside. So, just as the United States goes through great measures to protect their treasure, so you should also take great measures in guarding your heart, which is your treasure. Remember, vaults are designed to protect its contents from "theft and unauthorized use"; and surely, your heart is a treasure worth protecting, and being guarded from intruders, thieves, assassins, and users. It is far more valuable than all of the gold in Fort Knox. Therefore, don't allow just anyone in your "secret place"... guard it... because that's where YOUR treasure is, and everyone is not destined to have access to it.

Now, the vault concept is not a new one. When we look at the Old Testament, we see that the Tabernacle of the Lord had the outer court, the inner court, and the Holy of Holies. The outer court, in this instance, represents our physical bodies. This is what we present to the world. We're identifiable by our "outer court" display. Next, we have the inner court. This level represents our souls, which is comprised of our mind, will, and emotions. This is the part of our being that many of our friends and family are familiar with. The inner court is more intimate than the outer court portion of our being. There is familiarity and relationship on this level. This level goes beyond just the physical shell, but is a part of the inner you, thus the "inner court." Last, but certainly not least, there is the Holy of Holies. This is the most precious portion of your being. This is your spirit man. This is the vault. In the tabernacle, any common Israelite could enter the courts but only the priestly tribe could go beyond and into the Tabernacle. In addition, only the high priest could go beyond still into the Holy of Holies once per year on Yom Kippur, The Day of Atonement. However, today as born again believers, we have access to this special place, through Jesus' blood and sacrifice on the cross, as the veil was torn from the top down: "The curtain of the temple was torn in two from top to bottom." Mark 15:38

One of the reasons that the veil being torn from top to bottom is so significant is because it lets us know that God did it, as NO MAN could tear that curtain from the top! It was God's doing in order to allow His people access to His heart without a mediator, and to His throne of grace. This is why He now tells us to come boldly, with whatever's on our hearts or minds; because through Christ Jesus, we've been reconciled back to the Father, by the Holy Spirit:

"Let us therefore come boldly unto the throne of grace, that we may obtain mercy, and find grace to help in time of need." Hebrews 4:16 (KJV)

To approach anyone boldly, assumes much confidence. This is how God wants us to come to Him, as we are sons and daughters; not bastards. So it should be with the spouse that God ordains for our lives. When God tears the veils of the hearts of two individuals, from top to bottom, those two people are then knit together as one. Contrary to popular opinion, physical intimacy is the "outer court" of intimacy. In other words, that is not all there is, there's so much more, as "outer court" intimacy barely scratches the surface of what true intimacy is really about. This is why a man can sleep with a woman and never call her again. This is also why a man is able to have regular sex with a woman, yet never let her into his heart. This is evidenced when she asks questions like, "Why won't you talk to me?" or, "Why don't you open up to me?" The reason this occurs in many cases is because they've only connected on the outer court level; and if that physical experience is not sealed by the emotional and spiritual bond of intimacy that only comes through marriage, then the woman (and even the man at times) is sure to experience a feeling of emptiness. The next level of intimacy, of course, is the "inner court." This is where two people have a genuine interest in one another. They begin to share their likes and dislikes, future hopes, and dreams. In this place, they make each other laugh, and gaze into one another's eyes. It is in this place that they realize whether or not they want more of this person. So it's here that they'll decide if it's worth the effort to go deeper, stay where they are, or leave the inner court altogether. The problem sometimes with desiring to go to the next level is that many are not sure of how to go about getting there. In some instances, due to

traumatic or hurtful past experiences, some
purposely back away from exploring anything
further because of the fear of being hurt or rejected.
So, although many get to the inner court level, they
end up staying right there... even in marriage,
unfortunately. However, God ordained marriage to
be an experience of oneness, and without division:
"and the two will become one flesh. So they are no
longer two, but one." Mark 10:8 9

True intimacy occurs on the level of the Holy of
Holies. Even as believers, we must be born again in
order to get to this level of intimacy with the Lord,
as those who worship Him must worship Him in
spirit and in truth: "God is spirit, and his
worshipers must worship in spirit and in truth."
John 4:24

Because God is spirit, the only way that we can
truly worship Him is in spirit and in truth.
Therefore, we cannot worship Him from the outer
court (flesh), nor can we worship Him from the
inner court (mind and soul), but we must worship
Him from the most holy place; the Holy of Holies,

our spirit man. This is the only acceptable form of worship, Spirit to spirit. Now, in order for a husband and wife to truly become one on all levels, they must be of: (1) ONE Body... consummation of marriage; (2) ONE Mind... walking in agreement; (3) ONE Heart... loving, worshiping and serving the Lord Jesus Christ, the Great I AM.

True intimacy occurs between a man and woman when God has torn the veils of their hearts from the top down, towards one another. In essence, the Lord lets us know that He has put His stamp of approval on this person's life for you; and you for them. The torn veil represents safety. It also represents intimacy. The torn veil lets us know that this is an individual that you can TRUST with your innermost thoughts, desires, struggles, and fears; as well as the confidence to know that even after revealing this information to that person, they'll hold it... cherish it... protect it... and treat it as dearly as you would. When God tears that veil, it lets us know that this place is indeed a safe haven. Our heart is safe with this person; and theirs is safe with us. The virtuous woman understands this concept very well:

Who can find a virtuous woman? For her price is far above rubies. The heart of her husband doth safely trust in her, so that he shall have no need of spoil. She will do him good and not evil all the days of her life. Proverbs 31:10-12 (KJV)

The woman with whom a man trusts with his heart is called virtuous. Why would a man safely trust his heart to a woman of virtue? Keep in mind, the Proverbs 31 woman is never described by her flesh in any way; but by the fact that she is virtuous and full of wisdom. So what is virtue? We often hear the word tossed around, but what does it really mean? Virtue: moral excellence, goodness and righteous-ness; as well as an "effective force", "power or potency."

Thus, the woman who earns a man's trust with his heart, his prized hidden possession, must be one who is morally excellent, good, righteous, and an effective force with power and potency! In short, the virtuous woman is a bad woman... she's got it going on! She's not idle, but busy being productive... taking care of hubby, home, family and business!

She riseth also while it is yet night, and giveth meat to her household, and a portion to her maidens. She considereth a field, and buyeth it: with the fruit of her hands she planteth a vineyard. She girdeth her loins with strength, and strengtheneth her arms. She perceiveth that her merchandise is good: her candle goeth not out by night. She layeth her hands to the spindle, and her hands hold the distaff. Proverbs 31:15-19 (KJV)

The woman of virtue doesn't skip a beat, and her husband knows that although he is the head of the home, and of her life, that she is in fact the "neck." Her actions will typically determine the climate of her marriage, as well as her home. She has a power that is not loud, yet confident. She also has an unspoken ability to set the tone of her home. Women, please know that your power is not in how much you can over talk your man, nor is it in the fact that you may make more money than he does, nor is it in the fact that you may even have more education than he does; because at the end of the day, none of those things really matter, as there are plenty of beautiful, educated, professional sisters who are single, yet hoping to one day be married. So the key to having and keeping a happy husband and home is not measured by external accomplishments, but rather in your ability to respect your husband as the head. This is where it begins, as obedience is always better than sacrifice. Remember that Vashti refused the king's command to simply "come to him," and because of her blatant disrespect, dishonor, and   disobedience, the result was that she lost her position as Queen:

Queen Vashti also gave a banquet for the women in the royal palace of King Xerxes. On the seventh day, when King Xerxes was in high spirits from wine, he commanded the seven eunuchs who served him—Mehuman, Biztha, Harbona, Bigtha, Abagtha, Zethar and Carcas— to bring before him Queen Vashti, wearing her royal crown, in order to display her beauty to the people and nobles, for she was lovely to look at. But when the attendants delivered the king's command, Queen Vashti refused to come.

Then the king became furious and burned with anger. Esther 1:9-12

What on earth was wrong with Queen Vashti? Her husband, her king, simply called for her because he wanted to show off her beauty to his friends... and she refused. Wrong move! When someone has made you their queen, PLEASE treat them as a king; it's not difficult; really. More than anything, men need our respect. Respect is their love language.

A well-known singer once said it this way, "R-E-S-P-E-C-T, find out what it means to me!" Do not publicly (or privately) dis-respect the man that God has put in, and assigned to your life. Love your husband by respecting him, and do not do anything to him that you would not want done to you. Submitting to him equals RESPECTING him.

Now, Vashti's replacement, Esther, was respectful, obedient and honorable. We should never let our "position" in the Kingdom make us forget that we're here to serve the King, as being high in position is never a pass to be haughty, but rather, to exercise a greater level of humility. Esther understood the significance of this:

Now the king was attracted to Esther more than to any of the other women, and she won his favor and approval more than any of the other virgins. So he set a royal crown on her head and made her queen instead of Vashti. And the king gave a great banquet, Esther's banquet, for all his nobles and officials. He proclaimed a holiday throughout the provinces and distributed gifts with royal liberality. Esther 2:17-18

What's really important to be noted in this analogy is how many treat the King of kings, Jesus Christ, when He calls... calls us to pray, calls us to give, calls us to hold our tongue, calls us to stop doing some things, calls us to go... and sin no more, etc. The bottom line is, disobedience has a price attached to it and in Vashti's case, it cost her being Queen; because no matter how "beautiful" Esther may have been, she would not have even been an option had Vashti submitted to the king's will and did what she was supposed to do. Ask the Lord for the grace to be clothed in humility, as we must remember that meekness does not equal weakness. Walk in wisdom.... and don't allow reckless words and actions to wreck your relationships: "Therefore, as God's chosen people, holy and dearly loved, clothe yourselves with compassion, kindness, humility, gentleness, and patience." Colossians 3:12

Preparing for The Promise

Recently, I've been organizing and rearranging my closet, cleaning and getting rid of old clothes, as most of us do. I did this partly because it needed to be done, but also because I realized that if I am expecting my promise from the Lord, it's my job to prepare for it, and not just talk about it. When Esther waited for the promise to manifest, she didn't sit idly by, twiddling her thumbs... She prepared herself!

Before a girl's turn came to go in to King Xerxes, she had to complete twelve months of beauty treatments prescribed for the women, six months with oil of myrrh and six with perfumes and cosmetics. And this is how she would go to the king: Anything she wanted was given her to take with her from the harem to the king's palace. In the evening she would go there and in the morning return to another part of the harem to the care of Shaashgaz, the king's eunuch who was in charge of the concubines. She would not return to the king unless he was pleased with her and summoned her by name.

When the turn came for Esther (the girl Mordecai had adopted, the daughter of his uncle Abihail) to go to the king, she asked for nothing other than what Hegai, the king's eunuch who was in charge of the harem, suggested. And Esther won the favor of everyone who saw her. She was taken to King Xerxes in the royal residence in the tenth month, the month of Tebeth, in the seventh year of his reign.
Esther 2: 12-16

Please know that waiting for the promise involves action! "Show me your faith without works... and I'll show you my faith BY my works!" (James 2:18b; emphasis mine.) You want to prepare, because as long as you've been trusting and obeying the Lord, and you know by faith that what God has promised you is in route, you want to make absolutely certain that you're ready. Thus, preparation is key.

Now, although we see that Esther had physical beauty treatments, which are important, what we also need to remember is that spiritual and mental preparation is key as well. Understand that becoming one with the man that God has for you is not just about a wedding ceremony and reception, but rather knowing that you will become one with another individual. You, bone of his bone and flesh of his flesh, will now become one with him. So of course that takes preparation, and for anyone who is serious about their marriage, not just their wedding day, will understand the significance of preparing to minister, through marriage, to the one whom will be called husband.

Pumpernickel Bread & Rainbow Lollipops

Some people will argue that you can marry, and be compatible with anyone who has the characteristics of the type of person you're looking for. For example, as long as they're tall, dark, handsome, ambitious, kind, loving, generous, God-fearing, God-loving, etc. that you could marry, and be happy with anyone who has those particular characteristics. Now as great as that may sound on the surface, I would have to disagree; as saying that would be the equivalent of saying a turkey and Swiss sandwich on Rye bread is the same as a turkey and Swiss sandwich on pumpernickel bread. Although the contents may be the same, the entire dynamic of the sandwich changes because of the different types of bread. In addition, if you choose to have a rainbow lollipop for dessert (sweet) as opposed to a bag of barbeque potato chips (salty), this too will change the dynamic of the entire meal. This is why it is so important to wait on God for your mate, and see whom He has for you:

But for Adam, no suitable helper was found. So the Lord God caused the man to fall into a deep sleep; and while he was sleeping, he took one of the man's ribs and closed up the place with flesh. Then the Lord God made a woman from the rib he had taken out of the man, and he brought her to the man. The man said, "This is now bone of my bones and flesh of my flesh; she shall be called 'woman,' for she was taken out of man." For this reason a man will leave his father and mother and be united to his wife, and they will become one flesh. The man and his wife were both naked, and they felt no shame. Genesis 2:20b-25

The beauty of waiting on the Lord and allowing Him to bring you to the person that He has destined for you, is that He knits the two together in the spirit and therefore, they will have the ability to be "naked and not ashamed" before one another... spiritually, mentally, emotionally, and physically. This is possible because when the Lord does it, it will always be a perfect, purposeful fit.

Now, does that mean that the marriage will never have any problems? Of course not. However, what it does mean is that the man God has for you will be graced to love you the right way... and you will be graced to submit to him, as unto the Lord. Please know, the man you're looking at may have success, money, looks, charm, charisma... and he may even a relationship with the Lord... however, if he hasn't been given the grace to love you the "right" way, and the grace be in a covenant relationship with you... then you are surely building your house on sand. Wait on the Lord for your mate, because when God sends him... He will also equip him with everything he needs to love, honor, cherish and cover you. Everyone is not graced for you. Please know that. In other words, just because he's single, saved and successful, doesn't necessarily make him a potential husband for you!

In addition, when we look at the fact that the Lord took a rib out of Adam's side to form the woman, we need to understand that the rib taken from Adam is the only rib that will fit back into

Adam's rib cage. Many times, we see people trying to force relationships, when in fact, the one rib, the perfect rib, the rib taken out of the side of the man...will perfectly fit back into the man. Now, does this mean that other ribs won't be able to function inside of his rib cage? Absolutely not. However, any other rib will need some major adjusting, altering, etc. in order to "fit" as it is not the original rib of that man; and so it is with marriage. Many argue that we have the free will to marry whom we will, which is true. However, when we submit that free will to the perfect will of God, and say to the Lord, "Lord, this is who I want, but nevertheless, not my will, thy will be done...," that is when we allow the Lord to reveal to us whom He has for us. Remember, He knows us better than we know ourselves... so much so, that even the very hairs on our heads are not just counted... but numbered: "Indeed, the very hairs of your head are all numbered. Don't be afraid;" Luke 12:7a

Finally, please remember that just as square pegs do not fit into round holes, not just "any rib" will fit back into Adam's ribcage. So, do not try to force yourself to fit into the life of someone you were never ordained to be with! By the time you carve a little bit here, and a little bit there....making so many unnecessary adjustments... you won't even look like

yourself! So why force it? Don't you know the one God has for you will "fit you like a glove?" Just wait on the Lord, because the one He's preparing for you needs you without the major modifications! Trust Him, and let patience have her perfect work! If he leaves because of who you really are, then please do yourself a favor, and let him go. It's the best thing for both! No one should have to live as though they're walking on eggshells, trying to "please" someone who may have more interest in being controlling and manipulative, than they do in you. Be free! The Lord knows exactly who and what's needed for your life; and He's so faithful. If you win that man by becoming what he wants you to be, then when will you ever be free to be you? How long can you live like that? Seriously. To thine own self, be true! If it is God's will for you to be married, wait on Him to send you whom He has for you; and while you wait, focus on the Lord, keep Him first, delight yourself in Him, and work on you! Wait on Him, and be anxious for nothing!

"Be anxious for nothing, but in everything by prayer and supplication, with thanksgiving, let your requests be made known to God;" Philippians 4:6

No More Looking for LOVE in All the Wrong Places

When women haven't experienced the love of their earthly fathers, they often find themselves looking for love in all of the wrong places. So, they'll try to fill that void anyway they can... through sex, tolerating abusive relationships, embracing and nurturing low self-esteem through wearing provocative clothing in attempts to draw attention, etc. However, please know that a man will never fill that void in your heart. Even in the best of relationships and marriages, flesh is not capable of filling a heart's void. Only Jesus can! You don't need anyone to validate your worth when in Christ, He validated you on Calvary!

Mary J. Blige's song, "Father In You," clearly illustrates how so many women are looking for daddy's love through a man. Because daddy was never there physically, or even perhaps emotionally and spiritually, many women today end up longing for that "father figure" in whom they desire to call "their man." This level of expectation of a woman, from her man, is a recipe for great disappointment. If you're unfamiliar with the song, the lyrics are as follows:

When I was a little girl
I didn't have a father
And that's why I'm leaning on you..
When I was a baby
I didn't get a hug from daddy
That's why I need a hug from you..

Oh, It's not easy and
I thank you for putting up with me
When you don't have a daddy's love

To say that you...
To say that I'm your little girl
(Are his little girl, Oh why didn't you love me)
And give you the love..(I need love, yeah, yeah, yeah)

you really deserve (And I believe I deserve it And that's why)

[chorus]
That's why I need, The father in you
(I need the father in you, baby)
That's why I need, (Please don't hurt me please)
The father in you
That's why I need (Oh that's why)
The father in you (Really need you)
That's why I need (Please be true)
The father in you

Oh, things got bad, to the point
Where mommy couldn't hold us down
And that's when it hurt me so much
To see her, To see her cry
(Oh don't cry, momma don't cry momma)
Each and every night
(We're gonna be alright that's what I used to say)
I said that some day
That I would try to take his place
But it was too hard;

It was so hard trying to be a man and a woman
And that's why I need the father in you

[chorus]
That's why I need, (oh I needed)
The father in you, (I put my trust on you)
That's why I need, (Please don't let me down)
The father in you.
That's why I need,
The father in you (I need the father in you)
That's why I need (Hold my hand)
The father in you

Because we never had one at home
(No, No, No) As a little girl...
So I understand, why daddy couldn't be there
Cause it's so obvious nobody taught him, how to
be father to me
Oh and I'm not saying this
to reminisce on the past
I'm just saying this to make you understand, That
I needed a father
And this is my problem

This is why I couldn't keep no one
This is why I couldn't stay alone
I was so scared alone
Every woman needs a man
And I don't think she understands
That she really needs a father
The father in you, my brother
She really needed the father
The father in you.
When your wife is speaking fellas
Pay attention. Yeah, don't ignore her
No,no,no I really need the father in you. ~Mary J.
Blige

Believing that your husband is equipped to give you what your earthly father didn't, is a set-up for disaster. The fact that any woman would "need" a man to "father" her is proof of the real need for healing and wholeness, which can only be found in Christ Jesus. He is the Only One who is able to heal those deep places, and make you completely whole. David said it this way, "When my father and my mother forsake me, then the LORD will take me up." Psalm 27:10 (KJV)

David understood and had come to a place of peace in understanding, that when all others had forsaken him, even his parents, that the Lord Himself would receive Him as His very own. David did not lean on, nor depend on the arm of flesh to fill him in this way, or mend his broken heart. Rather, he used his brokenness as an opportunity to trust in the Lord even more, and believed that God would fill the empty places in his heart, while mending his brokenness. Remember, the Lord is near to those who are broken in their heart and spirit:

The righteous cry, and the LORD heareth, and delivereth them out of all their troubles. The LORD is nigh unto them that are of a broken heart; and saveth such as be of a contrite spirit. Psalm 34:17-18 (KJV)

Love's Ministry

No ministry will ever be complete without pain. It's through difficulties, through the pressing and through the squeezing of life's experiences that the anointing is produced; and it is the anointing that destroys the yokes of bondage. The first step to ministering with the anointing is being filled with the Holy Spirit. Then, as one begins to obey God's perfect will, one becomes more entrusted with the anointing. We are never commanded to be more anointed, nor are we corrected for not being powerful enough. However, we are told to obey. The anointing is God's job, not ours; and it is not anything that can ever be produced in the flesh. It only comes through a real relationship with the Father, through Jesus Christ, by the Holy Ghost; and obedience to His Word. God anoints those whom He appoints, as they humbly submit to His will in obedience. So please don't believe the hype, as in order for ministry to truly be effective, one must have gone through something that causes them to be able to relate to what others are going through; and have compassion. Just look at Jesus, He knows exactly what we go through, and struggle with, because He, too, was tempted in every way, yet without sin:

"For we do not have a high priest who is unable to sympathize with our weaknesses, but we have one who has been tempted in every way, just as we are--yet was without sin." Hebrews 4:15

Do you think if there was any other way for Him to save us from our sins, besides going to Calvary, He would have bled, suffered, and died? Jesus went to the cross for us because His love for us is so great that He did whatever was necessary in order to reconcile us back to the Father. So, it is with love. When you truly love, there will be good times, happiness and joy. However, in most cases, there will also be sacrifice, pain and hurt. Otherwise, how will you measure that it was in fact love?

The HURTING side of LOVE: AGAPE

Agape love has been defined as "the love that consumes," i.e., the highest and purest form of love, one that surpasses all other types of affection. I would have to agree with that definition. However, there is more to this kind of love. It's an unusual love. It is not the kind of love we immediately think of when love comes to mind. The moment you speak of love, most people automatically think of romance; or the type of love one would have for a child or friend. However, Agape truly supersedes all of that. It is the most unselfish, purest form of love that exists... so much so, that the Word of God tells us that "perfect love cast out fear," and "love covers a multitude of sins." So, I ask, what manner of love is this that can cast out fear and cover a multitude of sins? What manner of love is this that would cause the Father to give His only begotten Son... that whosoever believes in Him, should not perish, but have everlasting life? What manner of love is this?

Do you really believe that love doesn't hurt, nor ever will? Now, let's get one thing straight. I am not talking about abuse, or allowing someone to abuse, hurt, manipulate, or control you... physically, emotional, mentally, verbally, or otherwise. Not at all! Abuse does not equal love in any way, shape or form! I'm talking about real, authentic, genuine love; agape love, a term many throw around loosely but never truly grasp. It is the love that the Father has for us, through His Son Jesus. There is nothing erotic about this love (eros) nor, does it have pre-requisites for giving (philos). It just does what it does because it is love. It is love in its purest form. The Word of God declares, "For God so loved the world, He gave His Only Begotten son that whosoever believeth in Him, should not perish, but have everlasting life." John 3:16 (KJV, emphasis mine.) So, what does this really mean? What does God giving His only begotten Son to us mean? His only begotten that's been with Him from the very beginning; His only begotten who is sinless, and is the splitting image of His Father! "He who has seen me, has seen the Father." John 14:9

So, what manner of love is this, how the Father loves us so? Do you know the heart of the Father?

Do you know the tenderness of His heart? Do you know how much it must have hurt Him to give His only begotten for you and for me? Even Jesus cried, while on the cross, "Father, why hast thou forsaken me?", as He carried the sins of the entire world on His back. Some believe that God had to turn His back on Jesus while on the cross, because He carried the sins of the world; however I don't believe that, as it is not the nature of God to "turn"; for there is no shadow of turning in Him. Not to mention, He would never turn His back on His Only begotten Son. I believe He didn't answer Jesus because He was crying. I believe He was weeping. Just as Jesus wept at the death of Lazarus, so I believe the Father wept at the death of His Son. The evidence of the tears and pain were manifest after Jesus said, "It is finished," and gave up the ghost. At that moment, it began to rain profusely, and an earthquake took place. Then, the veil in the temple was torn from top to bottom, indicating it was indeed finished; and as painful and hurtful as it was to see His only Son bleed and die on that old rugged cross, it was all worth it; because as a result of the death, burial and resurrection of Jesus, many sons were passed from death to life! Hallelujah!

Therefore, just as sin entered the world through one man, and death through sin, and in this way death came to all men, because all sinned— for before the law was given, sin was in the world. But sin is not taken into account when there is no law. Nevertheless, death reigned from the time of Adam to the time of Moses, even over those who did not sin by breaking a command, as did Adam, who was a pattern of the one to come. But the gift is not like the trespass. For if the many died by the trespass of the one man, how much more did God's grace and the gift that came by the grace of the one man, Jesus Christ, overflow to the many! Again, the gift of God is not like the result of the one man's sin: The judgment followed one sin and brought condemnation, but the gift followed many trespasses and brought justification. For if, by the trespass of the one man, death reigned through that one man, how much more will those who receive God's abundant provision of grace and of the gift of righteousness reign in life through the one man, Jesus Christ. Consequently, just as the result of one trespass was condemnation for all men, so also the result of one act of righteousness was justification that brings life for all men. For just as through the disobedience of the one man the many were made sinners, so also through the obedience of the one man the many will be made righteous. (Romans 5:12-19)

This Agape love, loves through joy, through pain, through disappointment, and through hurt. This love, loves the unlovable. This love, loves even when it is not loved back. This is the hurting side of love. Agape love doesn't turn its back on the object of its love. It is the purest form of love. It is the only way to truly love. It is unconditional. It is the way the Father loves us. This is the love required for us to "love our enemies," as Jesus tells us to do. This is the love required for us to "pray for those who despitefully use and persecute us." This is the love that will cause us to live right, and live holy, as He admonishes us, "be ye holy, for I am holy." This is the love, when displayed, and walked in, will identify us, as His.

"A new command I give you: Love one another as I have loved you, so you must love one another. By this all men will know that you are my disciples, if you love one another." John 13:34-35

Does our love look like His love? If not, what does it look like?

LOVE is NOT SELFISH... but Sacrifices... by the fuel of obedience!

For God so loved the world... He gave His only begotten Son; that whosoever believeth in Him should not perish, but have eternal life. (John 3:16) So, let's look at this verse a little more closely... God's love is predicated by His giving. Because He loved us, He gave! Next, He didn't just give us anything... He gave us His very best! He gave us His Only begotten Son... Jesus, begotten directly of Him! His only Son that has been with Him since the beginning! His Son, who was there with Him since before the foundations of the world, His only begotten... and His best. Furthermore, Jesus's love for us was displayed through His obedience: "And being found in fashion as a man, he humbled himself, and became obedient unto death, even the death of the cross." Philippians 2:8. So, when we see God's love demonstrated, we see that He gave. He gave His only. He gave His best. Herein lies what love truly is. Therefore, when a man tells you that he loves you, be sure that his love for you resembles the Father's love. Make sure his proposed love is evident not just in word, but in deed; as the word declares that husbands are to love their wives as Christ loves His church... and died for it! So a husband should love His wife with the same tenacity, gentleness, sacrifice and selflessness as Christ loves His church, and even be willing to die for her; meaning to put her first, and never leave her alone, unprotected, or uncovered. Does this mean that the wife has no responsibility to her husband in marriage? Absolutely not! She is to submit to him, as unto the Lord. Submission, otherwise known as respect, is his love language. So, just as women need their husbands to love them, and be gentle with them; husbands need their wives to respect them. Because once the respect is gone, the heart usually follows. So, wives.... Please respect your husbands, as this is how he will know you truly love him. Respect, not lip service, is his love language. *"Wives, submit to your husbands, as is fitting in the Lord." Colossians 3:18*

Valley Girls: The DECEPTION of Delilah... Watch Out!!!

Delilah was a woman with outward beauty, a sketchy past, and an ulterior motive. She was seductive, sly, and persuasive, had charm, and used what she had in all of the wrong ways. Samson fell in love with Delilah, as the Word of God declares, "Sometime later, he fell in love with a woman in the Valley of Sorek whose name was Delilah."(Judges 16:4) Try to avoid falling in love with someone while they are in their valley. It's important to first find out if they are just passing through, or if they have taken up residence. Do they have a desire to leave, or are they comfortable staying? I'm not saying not to love them. However, use wisdom in giving them the time and space necessary to navigate properly through this critical chapter of their life. Sometimes, the Lord will have us in the valley for a purpose, a season or a reason. So, when we meet people in their valleys, sometimes, it's just important to step back, pray, and allow the Lord to deal with them during this season. The main thing is to let the Lord lead you, and not mistake a test, or ministry opportunity for what appears to be a potential marriage opportunity... as these are completely different things.   David said, "Yea, though I walk through the valley of the shadow of death, I will fear no evil"! (Psalm 23:4a, [KJV] emphasis mine.) Even David found himself walking through the valley, which lets us know that the valley is not a permanent residence, but designed to get us from "here" to "there."   So if you meet someone whose residence is the valley, stop... and ask the Lord to show you their purpose for your life; if any at all.   You were not destined to live in a valley, but to walk through it!

Next, the Word of God declares that Delilah was "a woman of the valley." We are also told that she *lived there.* This was a woman who clearly had no intention of moving forward, or out. She liked the valley.   This was clearly a woman who was complacent in her circumstances and current condition; and erroneously assumed that money could change her mentality. This was a woman who apparently did not have enough vision to be able to see that she was in a valley, so she called it her home. Be careful of falling in love with those who call the valley their home. This is a person of limited vision, limited faith, and typically full of fear. Be careful of the "valley residents," because while you are "walking through" they will try to tempt, or trick you into staying. They will try to convince you that the valley is "where it's at," and where you belong... but the devil is a liar!

Furthermore, this woman from the valley had connections with Samson's enemies, as they were confident enough to know they could utilize and depend on her, to do their dirty work:

The rulers of the Philistines went to her and said, "See if you can lure him into showing you the secret of his great strength and how we can overpower him so we may tie him up and subdue him. Each one of us will give you eleven hundred shekels of silver." So Delilah said to Samson, "Tell me the secret of your great strength and how you can be tied up and subdued." Judges 16:5-6

I find it interesting that Samson's enemies knew they could count on Delilah. They knew her price, which implies this wasn't her first assignment. She didn't try to negotiate, she just agreed. Be careful of the "valley residents"... they will sell you out cheap!

Uncomplicated Love

We think that love is a complicated thing, but it isn't. It is as simple as doing for others what you would want done for you; and treating someone the same way that you would want to be treated. Love is no respecter of persons; it just does. So, if the next thing you say or do, no matter how big or small isn't something you would want returned to you, then don't do it. Loving one another is how men know that we are truly His disciples. It is not about how loud we shout, how pious we appear, how many tongues we speak, how many scriptures we know, or how many prophetic words we have given. At the end of the day, we are known by our fruit, not our gifts! Remember, the gifts of the Spirit are without repentance. In other words, God is not an Indian giver. So, once He gives someone a gift, He doesn't take it back. "For the gifts and calling of God are without repentance." Romans 11:29 (KJV)

It is also important to understand that the possession of a gift(s) does not always indicate the presence of God resting in, and on an individual's life.   Please be discerning,   and never just get caught up in how well someone preaches, sings, heals, prophesies, works miracles, etc... because gifted does not equal anointed.   To anoint is to pour, or smear with oil; thus those who are truly anointed by God are not just recognizable by mere gifts... but by the smearing on of God's presence on their lives; as His Spirit produces His fruit. This is also why one should never get all caught up in someone's title without first examining their fruit! Fruit will always tell the real story, as Jesus said... it is by their fruit that we will know them. "But the fruit of the Spirit is love, joy, peace, patience, kindness, goodness, faithfulness, gentleness and self-control. Against such things there is no law." Galatians 5:22-23

Is the fruit of the Spirit (the evidence of God's presence) manifest in their lives?   Are they kind? (fruit)... Are they loving? (fruit)... Are they patient? (fruit)... Do they have self-control? (fruit)... Are they good? (fruit)... Are they joyful? (fruit)... Are they faithful? (fruit)... Are they gentle? (fruit)... Are they peaceful? (fruit)

Furthermore, having a title does not guarantee the anointing of God, nor does the anointing of God guarantee a title! So please do not get caught up in thinking that you have to marry a Pastor, Bishop, Apostle, Elder, etc. as if just because a man carries a title, that it guarantees that he also carries God's Spirit... it does not. Now, although there are some genuine men of God who carry titles, please understand that a title will never guarantee the authenticity of that man. Once again, know him by his fruit. When the Lord anoints, there are no Xerox® machines present! So, please be sure to watch for fruit (love, joy, peace, kindness, self-control, patience, etc...,) as there is a BIG difference between a "copy" and original ink!

Finally, if you've discovered that they have a track record or pattern of questionable behavior, what makes you think that they will be any different with you? Track records are proof (fruit) of character, integrity, or the lack thereof. Therefore, just as a bank wouldn't lend money without first checking credit, why would you just give your heart away, without administering a spiritual background check? Try not to be so emotional. Watch, pray, be patient and while God is revealing to you who they really are, step back and let Him heal, and deal with them!

Some Will... Some Won't... So What!

People can be fickle! One day they like you, and the next day they don't! So never get caught up in thinking how someone feels about you has anything to do with who you are, or what God knows about you! Always know who and whose you are, and don't feed into the fickleness of others. Just know what it is, keep loving them (sometimes from afar) and keep it moving! Keep your eyes fixed on Jesus, and remember, you are fearfully and wonderfully made:

"I will praise thee; for I am fearfully and wonder-fully made: marvellous are thy works; and that my soul knoweth right well." Psalm 139:14 (KJV

The Battle of the Sexes... Tug-of-War Anyone?

As it pertains to relationships, please know that most men are hunters by nature, and love to do the pursuing... (I don't make the rules; I just know what they are.) Now, are there ever exceptions to the rule? Of course there are; however, they are just those... exceptions. I am sure that if you talked to 10 men, at least 8 would agree that they like to initiate going to the next level, while pursuing, or in a relationship. Now, please know, I am not speaking of having sex out of marriage, because if any man expects that from you without first marrying you, then he has illustrated his respect level for you. Here, I am talking about the desire to be in an exclusive relationship. This has nothing to do with being honest with how you feel; it has to do with allowing him to lead, as that should be his position, as the man. So, just as some men say, "We should be honest with our feelings," shouldn't those same men have enough courage to step up and express their feelings and desire to go to the next level? Biblically speaking, is this not proper order? Also, one may want to ask themselves these questions: "Why am I rushing?", "Am I being anxious...and if so, why?" "Why not let things flow naturally?"

Now as far as it "being ok" to love someone who doesn't love you back...while, I agree we are to love everyone, we are also to walk in wisdom! It's not wise to wear our hearts on our sleeves, as the Word tells us to, "Keep your heart with all diligence for out of it spring the issues of life." (Proverbs 4:23 [NKJV]) When we decide to let someone into that secret place... into our Holy of Holies... it will be because they've earned the right to be there and not because of emotions, butterflies, or "trial and error." Of course, to each his own... however, I know that for me, it is a must to know who belongs in the outer court, the inner court and the Holy of Holies of my life. When one decides that someone should move from "friendship only" to being in a relationship, it should not be based on emotions alone, but by whether or not the Holy Spirit has given the "green light" to move forward, letting us know it's safe to allow that person closer to our hearts. This is not about the fear of rejection, but truly knowing who to cast your pearls to.

Finally, this has nothing to do with playing games, but using wisdom, as no woman has to ever come off as appearing desperate or anxious, because the reality is when a man really wants a woman, there's nothing that will stop him from going after her. Jacob illustrates this perfectly when he told Laban that he would work for him for seven years in exchange for his daughter, Rachel, because of his love for her:

Now Laban had two daughters; the name of the older was Leah, and the name of the younger was Rachel. Leah had weak eyes, but Rachel was lovely in form, and beautiful. Jacob was in love with Rachel and said, "I'll work for you seven years in return for your younger daughter Rachel." Genesis 29:16-18

When a man truly wants you, there is nothing that can keep him from coming for, and to you. In other words, you don't have to lower your standards to attract, get, or keep a man; because it is your   standards that will cause him to step up to the plate and do whatever is necessary to win you. You're worth it!

Be his FRIEND first... You'll be so glad you did!

My grandmother would always say, "If you've got one good friend... you're blessed." True friends are real jewels. They love you when you don't love yourself. They love you when it seems you do not love them back. They do not treat the friendship like a business, or contract (with conditions), but they are there simply because they want to be. Unfortunately, many make the mistake of bypassing the development of this critical stage, with the anticipation of moving straight-way into a relationship! So, as a result, trust hasn't had the opportunity to be earned, nor has friendship had the chance to truly develop. Consequently, this is one of the reasons controlling behavior begins.

What you don't want to do...

Please don't make the mistake of blowing up his phone...calling him multiple times back to back, just because you can't reach him. Don't keep tabs on him, checking his pants pockets, anxious to find something that may not even be there. Although he may never express it verbally, he knows that real friends don't need to check his pockets, pat him down, and insult him with on-going interrogation sessions. Real friends also don't have to check-in with you every 5 minutes. It's understood that even if you don't speak multiple times a day, you're still friends. They are secure, and know that even when the seasons change, the friendship remains the same. They don't catch attitudes when things don't go their way. If you can relate to any of these, you may not be operating in the spirit of a friend, but instead, the spirit of control, and insecurity.

Sometimes, the best way to answer... is NOT to!

You don't have to win every argument, nor do you have to always have the last word. Please learn the power of silence... when appropriate. Typically, men do not respond to words, but they do respond to nonverbal communication. If you are having a disagreement with your significant other, please know that you don't have to win every battle. It's ok to just let some things go. Know when to just be quiet as a soft answer turns away wrath. Quite frankly, when we are raising our voices, debating and challenging in disrespectful manners and tones, most of what we say goes in one ear and out of the other anyway. So, why waste the time or the breath? My grandmother would always say, "If you can't say anything nice, then don't say anything at all." When your desire to win the argument outweighs your desire to demonstrate love, humility and kindness, you still may end up being the "Biggest

Loser"! Please do not lose the war because you are so busy trying to win the battle. It's not always worth it.

DON'T miss the forest for the trees!!!!

We often hear people say, "Hindsight is 20/20," however, why is that? Why is it so hard for some to appreciate what they have while they have it? If someone allows you entrance into the inner places of their life, don't take it for granted or treat it casually. Cherish that person and the respect they've shown you, because how you handle it will determine whether you stay or go, as "access granted" does not guarantee permanent residence.

The Promise or The Counterfeit?

D o not mistake your Isaac for Ishmael. They look alike, talk alike and act alike, but they're not alike! Open your spiritual eyes, as natural eyes cannot discern between the two. Watch and pray!

Abraham and Sarah desperately wanted a child, and although God promised they would have one, they allowed themselves to become anxious and felt they needed to "help the Lord out." Now, how many times have we done this? We do this due to lack of patience, a heart full of anxiety, and sometimes, just flat out disobedience. What we must remember is when God promises something to us, many times we don't have to put our hands in it; all we have to do is trust Him, obey Him, rest in Him and wait on Him. Nevertheless, in haste, Sarah called on her maidservant, Hagar; thinking that in doing so, she would be assisting God in bringing the promise to pass:

Now Sarai, Abram's wife, had borne him no children. But she had an Egyptian maidservant named Hagar; so she said to Abram, "The Lord has kept me from having children. Go, sleep with my maidservant; perhaps I can build a family through her."

Abram agreed to what Sarai said. So after Abram had been living in Canaan ten years, Sarai his wife took her Egyptian maidservant Hagar and gave her to her husband to be his wife. He slept with Hagar, and she conceived. Genesis 16:1-4a

Although Hagar conceived Ishmael, he was still not the child of promise; and in spite of fleshly efforts, the promise, which only comes by the Spirit, could not be produced. Next, in arranging all of this, what Sarah did not bank on was Hagar's shift in attitude. You see, Hagar was Sarah's handmaid, but after she became pregnant with Ishmael, she forgot her position and lost her manners:

When she knew she was pregnant, she began to despise her mistress. Then Sarai said to Abram, "You are responsible for the wrong I am suffering. I put my servant in your arms, and now that she knows she is pregnant, she despises me. May the Lord judge between you and me." "Your servant is in your hands," Abram said. "Do with her whatever you think best." Then Sarai mistreated Hagar; so she fled from her.

Genesis 16:4b-6

It is so critical that we understand not to try and "move God's hand" after He has promised something to us. We are to simply trust, obey and wait on Him.

The promise will not come by natural events, but can only be produced by God's hand... supernaturally! Wait on Him!

Abraham fell facedown; he laughed and said to himself, "Will a son be born to a man a hundred years old? Will Sarah bear a child at the age of ninety?" And Abraham said to God, "If only Ishmael might live under your blessing!"

Then God said, "Yes, but your wife Sarah will bear you a son, and you will call him Isaac. I will establish my covenant with him as an everlasting

covenant for his descendants after him. And as for
Ishmael, I have heard you: I will surely bless him; I
will make him fruitful and will greatly increase his
numbers. He will be the father of twelve rulers, and I
will make him into a great nation." Genesis 17:17-20

The promise cannot be manipulated or rushed,
nor can it be put together in the flesh. The promise
that God has for you will only come by faith,
obedience, and waiting on the Lord; as He said to
Abraham, "I am God Almighty; walk before me and
be blameless." Genesis 17:1b

Moving prematurely, ahead of what the Lord has
spoken may get you an Ishmael, but it will not get
you the Promise. The Lord is very clear about
through whom, and with whom, His covenant will
be established. "But my covenant I will establish
with Isaac, whom Sarah will bear to you by this
time next year."

Genesis 17:21

However, when you try to rush the promise, take matters into your own hands, operate in anxiety, refuse to wait on the Lord, and do it your own way... you run the risk of ending up with a wild, stubborn ass:

He will be a wild donkey of a man;

his hand will be against everyone

and everyone's hand against him,

and he will live in hostility

toward all his brothers. Genesis 16:12

God's blessing requires God's order!

We often hear believers and unbelievers alike ask for the blessing of the Lord; and although He rains on the just and the unjust, His blessing and favor only come by His order. In other words, if we want God to bless it, we must do it GOD'S WAY! So, what is the way of the Lord? What is His order? Unfortunately, many operate in relationships that are completely out of order, hoping for God to put His stamp of approval on it, when He never ordained it in the first place. Sorry, it just doesn't work that way. I know because that used to be me. At only 26 years old, I began believing the lie that I was "old" and needed to get married, and start a family. Well, I met someone. Ironically, I prayed about it first... yes, I said prayed. I had been saved for 6 years at this point. I was very specific about my prayers too. I prayed that he would be over 6 feet tall, and that he would have hazel eyes, in addition to being saved and loving God. Well, I want you to realize that God wasn't the only one who heard my prayers. It seemed that not long after I prayed that prayer, I had tall, brown-skinned brothers with light eyes approaching me from out of the woodwork! One even said loudly and publicly to me while in a car dealership, that he wanted me to be his wife. I knew that these men were not sent by God. I knew then that the devil had also heard my request.

Not long after that, I met another tall gentleman, about 6'2", also with hazel eyes. He was saved, hand-some, a hard worker and business owner... and even spoke in tongues. Boy, I just knew that he was the one; even though he had only been saved for only 6 months. However, the Lord had warned me 5 different times, through dreams and prophetic words, that he was not the one. I did not listen. I was disobedient, and we were married that same year. No, it wasn't a shotgun wedding; I wasn't pregnant, but I was being led emotionally, and being deceived at the same time.

Following the Spirit vs. following your emotions...can mean the difference between life and death.

The first thirty days of the marriage seemed like heaven. We were so romantic and loving towards one another. We would even get compliments from strangers about how well we looked together. Then something happened...and it was drastic. Late one night, after I had already washed the dishes, cleaned the kitchen, and was already in the bed, my now ex-husband went into the kitchen, and made himself a very late night bowl of cereal... Ok, no problem. He then left the bowl in the sink, and got in the bed to go to sleep. I then asked him, "Are you going to wash your bowl?" He knew that I liked my kitchen clean before I went to bed, which is why I washed the dishes. His response was, "I don't do dishes." Now, on the surface, this may not seem like a big deal. However, right before we were married, he would stand side-by-side with me, helping to wash and dry dishes as we talked, laughed, etc. At this moment, I realized that I didn't know this man. I also realized that I had married a stranger; and from that point on, the marriage became emotionally and physically abusive, until I got to a point where I felt like I was walking on eggshells. The morning after the last physical attack, which almost led to my death because of suffocation, I packed what little my son and I had (he was 7 months old at the time), and left. My premature, unauthorized marriage reminds me of Ishmael, the son of flesh; and how he was produced as a result of anxiety and haste:

"But he who was of the bondwoman was born after the flesh; but he of the freewoman was by promise."

Galatians 4:23 (KJV)

Wait... Pray... Worship...Obey

When Abram was ninety-nine years old, the LORD appeared to him and said, "I am God Almighty; walk before me and be blameless. I will confirm my covenant between me and you and will greatly increase your numbers." Abram fell facedown, and God said to him, Genesis 17:1-3

In other words, there was more after verse 2 that the Lord wanted to release to Abraham (See verses 4-22). The word released to Abraham from the Lord began in verses 1-3, however, there had to be a "pause" after verse 3, as the Bible says, "Abraham fell facedown, AND GOD SAID.....

How many times do we get a word from the Lord, and get so excited, because of the one or two words we've just received, that we IMMEDIATELY JUMP UP and want to call "mom-n-them, our Pastor, our friends, sister, brother or whomever? Some of us even go as far as running to Face Book or Twitter pages to post our "word" as a status, or somehow share it with others; however, Abraham did none of that. Right after the Lord began to speak to him, he worshiped and bowed down in reverence to the Lord; and after that moment, the meat of the word was released unto him:

"As for me, this is my covenant with you: You will be the father of many nations. No longer will you be called Abram; your name will be Abraham, for I have made you a father of many nations. I will make you very fruitful; I will make nations of you, and

kings will come from you. I will establish my covenant as an everlasting covenant between me and you and your descendants after you for the generations to come, to be your God and the God of your descendants after you. The whole land of Canaan, where you are now an alien, I will give as an everlasting possession to you and your descendants after you; and I will be their God."

Then God said to Abraham, "As for you, you must keep my covenant, you and your descendants after you for the generations to come. This is my covenant with you and your descendants after you, the covenant you are to keep: Every male among you shall be circumcised. You are to undergo circumcision, and it will be the sign of the covenant between me and you. For the generations to come every male among you who is eight days old must be circumcised, including those born in your household or bought with money from a foreigner—those who are not your offspring. Whether born in your household or bought with your money, they must be circumcised. My covenant in your flesh is to be an everlasting covenant. Any uncircumcised male, who has not been circumcised in the flesh, will be cut off from his people; he has broken my covenant."

God also said to Abraham, "As for Sarai your wife, you are no longer to call her Sarai; her name will be Sarah. I will bless her and will surely give you a son by her. I will bless her so that she will be the mother of nations; kings of peoples will come from her."

Abraham fell facedown; he laughed and said to himself, "Will a son be born to a man a hundred years old? Will Sarah bear a child at the age of ninety"? And Abraham said to God, "If only Ishmael might live under your blessing"!

Then God said, "Yes, but your wife Sarah will bear you a son, and you will call him Isaac. I will establish my covenant with him as an everlasting covenant for his descendants after him. And as for Ishmael, I have heard you: I will surely bless him; I will make him fruitful and will greatly increase his numbers. He will be the father of twelve rulers, and I will make him into a great nation. But my covenant I will establish with Isaac, whom Sarah will bear to you by this time next year." When he had finished speaking with Abraham, God went up from him.

Genesis 17:4-22

Why is this important?   This is significant because many times as the Lord begins to speak a word to us, instead of going into worship and reverencing Him for taking the time out to have that one-on-one intimate moment with us... we get SO excited, we simply want to race to the phones, and immediately recite to others the word we've just received from the Lord; YET not even being sure that we've even gotten the whole thing. So, not only did Abraham worship and reverence the Lord while the word was being released... the word also declares, that once God finished speaking to Abraham, He obeyed God on that same day!

God finished speaking to Abraham and then left. On that same day, Abraham obeyed God by circumcising Ishmael.   Abraham was also circumcised, and so were all other men and boys in his household, including his servants and slaves.
Genesis 17:22-25 (CEV)

When God makes you a promise, all you have to do is believe and obey Him. This is what Abraham did... He believed God, and it was counted to him as righteousness. What does this mean? The Lord was pleased that Abraham believed Him in spite of how impossible the promise seemed in the natural.

He took him outside and said, "Look up at the heavens and count the stars--if indeed you can count them," then He said to him, "So shall your offspring be." Abraham believed the Lord, and He credited it to him as righteousness. Genesis 15:5-6

Please know that to believe God and take Him at His word is just RIGHT, in and of itself, regardless of what it looks or feels like. If He said it, He will do it, as He is not a man that He should lie, nor the son of man that He should repent. So, whatever He says, it's got to come to pass! Faith is never based upon feelings or appearances, but faith in God is based on, "Do you believe God?" This is why we would often hear Jesus say, "According to thy faith, be it unto you." As the writer of Hebrews declares:

But without faith it is impossible to please him: for he that cometh to God must believe that he is, and that he is a rewarder of them that diligently seek him. Hebrews 11:6 (KJV)

Furthermore, the Lord is so serious about having faith in Him, that we see there were instances where few miracles were performed, due to lack of the people's faith:

Coming to his hometown, he began teaching the people in their synagogue, and they were amazed. "Where did this man get this wisdom and these miraculous powers"? they asked. "Isn't this the carpenter's son? Isn't his mother's name Mary, and aren't his brothers James, Joseph, Simon and Judas? Aren't all his sisters with us? Where then did this man get all these things?" And they took offense at him.

But Jesus said to them, "Only in his hometown and in his own house is a prophet without honor."

And he did not do many miracles there because of their lack of faith.

Matthew 13:54-58

When people allow themselves to get caught up in being concerned with your credentials, your pedigree, where you're from, who you know, who knows you, etc... and allow familiarity to breed contempt, they risk missing the miracle for their own lives. Don't miss out on your miracle because you never know how, or through whom the Lord may choose to deliver it.

Loving her as Christ loves His church... and died for it~

*H*usbands, love your wives, just as Christ loved the church and gave himself up for her to make her holy, cleansing her by the washing with water through the word, and to present her to himself as a radiant church, without stain or wrinkle or any other blemish, but holy and blameless. In this same way, husbands ought to love their wives as their own bodies. He who loves his wife loves himself. Ephesians 5:25-28

Is he, the prospective husband, truly equipped, pre-pared and anointed to love you as Christ loves His church? If not, then you will never experience true love through a man, the way it was intended to be. Wait on the one who fully understands this... not just in word, but in deed.

A man can love his wife so FULLY, as Christ loves the church and gave Himself for it. One example that comes to mind when I think about a man loving his wife in this way, is the story of

Hosea and Gomer. The Lord was the One who told Hosea to marry a woman like Gomer; therefore, their union was ordained by God, and it was not without purpose. Hosea was graced to be Gomer's husband in spite of her "issues." By the world's standards, He probably should not have married her, but he obeyed God. When it comes to marriage, it's important to first hear from God, because His 'yes' will ensure getting HIS grace which will be necessary for the relationship. Hosea's obedience to the Lord and level of commitment to his wife is something to be noted:

When the LORD began to speak through Hosea, the LORD said to him, "Go, take to yourself an adulterous wife and children of unfaithfulness, because the land is guilty of the vilest adultery in departing from the LORD." So he married Gomer daughter of Diblaim, and she conceived and bore him a son. Hosea 1:2-3

In regard to Christ and His church, the love of Jesus causes one to want to submit to Him. When we realize how much He truly loves us, and how many times we didn't get what we deserved (grace and mercy), you don't want to disappoint Him. Rather than grieving Him, you want to please Him! His love for you makes you want to submit. Not by force, but by will...by desire. The Lord wants us to love Him. He wants our affection. He wants our devotion, and sure, He could've "strong-armed" us into loving Him (as some unfortunately attempt to do, even within the Body of Christ) but He didn't. He could've even created us as robots so we would just do whatever He wanted us to do, but He didn't do that either. Christ's love for His church is a sacrificial love, and many today don't want to sacrifice. Christ laid His life down for His church; however, many today struggle with dying daily, and putting their flesh under subjection. There are some today, unfortunately, who are self-centered (this goes both ways.). For example, a husband may feel he can treat his wife as a piece of property, as opposed to treating her as a person; a woman with feelings, thoughts, and individuality. Many haven't even taken the time out to really get to know their wives... like, "what's her favorite color?" as an example, perhaps because it was really about him, and not them to begin with? A woman loves it when a man remembers the "little things," because it shows that he pays close attention to her, and he cares. Likewise, the Lord is intimate with His bride, and so should a husband be with his, but not just in the obvious way.

The Lord lets us know that it is with loving kindness that He draws us, and so it is (or should be) with husbands and wives. Although a woman's love for her man somewhat develops on its own, his love for her greatly factors in as well, especially when he walks in loving kindness, like his Lord. When that man truly loves his wife the right way, he won't have to ask or beg for her respect... she'll want to give it to him. Lack of submission won't be an issue in this man's marriage, because his love for her will make her want to submit to him. When a husband loves his wife as Christ loves His church, the love of Christ, through him, has the ability to heal and restore that woman... so there will be nothing missing or broken. Now, this is not to say that she shouldn't already be healed, and whole before going into marriage, as we shouldn't mistake being healed with being perfect; but rather to say that when God joins the two together, and they become one, there's another level of completeness in that.

Let him CHASE you!!!

Men who allow themselves to get caught by women who chase them only let themselves get caught for ONE REASON. Then, when they are done, they will chase for the woman they want to *KEEP*. ~ Emil Thomas

Never chase a man! Why? Because that will only make him quickly run in the opposite direction! Not to mention, a man of vision won't be focused on what's behind him anyway, but what's in front of him. So, instead of taking on the "hunter role," (i.e., Out of Order!) focus on chasing Jesus, delight yourself in Him, and as the word declares... in doing so, He will give you the desires of your heart. Keep Him first and wait on Him! Men are hunters by nature, so let him be just that... the hunter! Don't give in, wave the white towel, or play dead before the appointed time! Hunting is what he does; it's a part of his nature and it keeps the courtship, and relationship interesting. It also helps to develop the friendship, because after all, it is called the "thrill of the chase" and not the "thrill of the easily conquered"! Most men want what they can't have, so don't just hand him the keys, and give him free test drives without even knowing if he qualifies. Every time you allow him to drive off the lot, without even knowing if he's approved, your value depreciates... and YOU are way too valuable for that!

Therefore, stop expecting a formal, five-course meal when all you've been doing is accepting crumbs! Change your level of expectation, change your standard of acceptance, and you'll change your outcome! "As a man thinks in his heart, so is he." (Proverbs 23:7) Your expectation is materialized by what you will and won't accept. Don't settle for anything less than God's best for your life.

WAIT on the Lord!

But they that wait upon the LORD shall renew their strength; they shall mount up with wings as eagles; they shall run, and not be weary; and they shall walk, and not faint. Isaiah 40:31(KJV)

Waiting and developing patience is not a new concept to a child of God. However, waiting for the right bus at the wrong bus stop and the right plane at the wrong airport does nothing. For those waiting on husbands, consider that he may not even run in your current circles, but in the circles of the vision that God has given you. The sooner we get to work being about our Father's business, the sooner we can be found.

An Eagle... or some "other" fowl?

If you choose to continue participating in their drama, foolishness, and nursery rhyme activities, please don't be surprised when they're unable to identify you as an eagle, or a chicken! Eagles always fly high, above mess, and with lots of grace; so please, exit the coop quickly, and leave those chickens behind! You have a purpose to fulfill! You're not in a circus, so please stop jumping through their hoops! When the relationship is right, it will flow naturally, it will yield peace, there will be reciprocity, and you won't feel like you're often in a warzone, playing tug-of-war! Whatever you do, don't force it, as sometimes it's necessary to take a "step-back" in order to see the entire picture clearly. Furthermore, don't waste another breath reminding them that, "Tricks are for Kids" when you agreed to get into the sandbox with them in the first place. Rather, get up, shake the sand off, step out of the box.... and as you "depart in peace," tell them that you've long outgrown that game, you have no more interest, and you've graduated past building "sand castles," and playing "trivial pursuit"! Tell them "thank you," but "no thank you," and kindly give them the gift of "good-bye."

To forgive or not to forgive... THAT is the question...

Forgive, not just for them, but for you too. Forgiving someone doesn't necessarily mean letting them back into that personal, intimate space, but rather releasing that thing you're holding against them. This way, you can be free to love from a right heart and spirit. Don't allow unforgiveness to contaminate your ability to love again. Unforgiveness blocks "love's flow" to the heart; surprisingly, it's more than just one-way blockage. It blocks the flow of love going out, as well as the flow of love attempting to come in. Unforgivness will blur your vision to even be able to identify love; so please forgive, let it go, and don't miss love knocking at your heart's door! Many times when people harbor unforgiveness, it's usually due to some past hurt or experience that has deeply wounded their heart, and although they may have healed on their own, the scar tissue that covers the wound is always much coarser than the original, tender heart tissue. This is why it's so important to allow the Lord to truly heal us when we've been hurt. So often, after being wounded from a relationship, many immediately hop into another; expecting that next person to do for them what only God can do. Relationship hopping is not the answer, because all you end up doing is taking baggage (unresolved issues, unresolved hurt, unresolved pain) from one relationship, into the next, and into the next again... yet, with no results.

It reminds me of the woman Jesus met at the well, who was experienced in relationship hopping, until she met the ONE who quenched her thirst, and satisfied her longings:

He told her, "Go, call your husband and come back." "I have no husband," she replied. Jesus said to her, "You are right when you say you have no husband. The fact is, you have had five husbands, and the man you now have is not your husband. What you have just said is quite true." John 4:16-18.

Then, leaving her water jar, the woman went back to the town and said to the people, "Come, see a man who told me everything I ever did. Could this be the Christ?" They came out of the town and made their way toward him. John 4:28-30

Allowing the Lord to heal you is the key to wholeness and it's ok to not be with someone for a season, as even sick people in the hospital need time to fully recover before going home. You don't have to be the walking wounded, for there is a balm in Gilead! Please allow Jesus to heal your heart, and brokenness. He is the only one who can.

You're NOT a yo-yo, so STOP letting him string you along!!!

As a kid, I really enjoyed amusement parks, and would always go straight to the roller coasters with the most speed, the steepest hills, and the most loops. However, as I've gotten older, all I can say to that now is "not so much anymore." Going to the parks are still great, however my appetite for entertainment and fun have definitely changed. Now, I'm sure roller coasters are still lots of fun for some adults; however, they are never any fun when they mirror your relationships. Please stop expecting stability while still agreeing to stay on the roller coaster. Have you ever noticed the names of some coasters? Cyclone, Hurler, Anaconda, Big Bad Wolf, Bizarro, Goliath, Prowler, Nemesis... and the list goes on. When it comes to your heart, and you know you're on a roller coaster... stop the ride, get off, and don't just exit the park... but shut it completely down! Your heart wasn't designed for constant "thrills" or abrupt "ups and downs." Don't just tolerate anything for the sake of pseudo-companionship, as clowns belong in a circus, NOT with you! Being humorous is one thing; however, being a joke is something altogether different. So, wait on the Lord, as He understands humor, but He won't send you a joker. You have come too far to make your life a laughing matter now! Let the clowns and jokers stay in the amusement park.

Next, refuse to be in anyone's stand-by line! Why? Because you don't have to! I mean, really... what kind of foolishness is that? I remember watching the show, "The Bachelor" and would think, "Why on earth would these women line up, and care about being chosen by a man who expects them to walk on eggshells, compete with numerous other women, and pretend to be perfect just to get him?" I don't get it. A man like that... they can keep! The man may do the "finding," but remember that you (along with the Holy Spirit) still do the choosing. So truly, it's ok to be selective, because when you truly understand who and whose you are, you will never wear the garb of desperation!

So, if this sounds like something you've endured, it's ok, as temporary blindness is not a travesty. However, you still need to open your eyes at some point. If you give them an inch, they will want an entire mile! Remember, your standards have been in place for a reason. Maintain them, and don't apologize for keeping them high. They're up there for a reason! In other words, know when it's time to keep it moving! Walk in wisdom!

All That GLITTERS is NOT gold...

Some packages are wrapped so beautifully, that we're sometimes careful about how we open them. We shouldn't just fall in love with the wrapping, but wait to discover its contents! Don't be so quick to love the covering, as you may be disappointed with what's inside! Also, don't always discount and discard packages wrapped in torn, plain, brown paper; as in doing so, you may be passing on a diamond in the rough! White-washed tombs may be beautiful on the outside, but can still be full of dead men's bones; whereas someone on fire for the Lord, and full of the Holy Ghost, may be overlooked because he doesn't have the "image," nor does he fit into the "clique." So, never be blinded by the jewelry, but always ask the Lord who is who!

Ok Lord, Ok... I give up... NOT my will, but your will be done~

J ust when you've finally made up your mind to surrender all to Christ without turning back, it seems like all hell breaks loose! You begin to experience attacks in areas, and on levels you never have before. I mean, you've had adversity before, but not quite like this. Your back is up against the wall, and you need God to move on your behalf like never before! Now, what I'm about to share is extremely significant... so take note. Please know that as a child of God who is living according to God's will, these are pivotal moments in your life. These strategic moments can either be the door to elevation, or proof that the current grade needs to be repeated! Don't you know that there's a series of tests for each level, and then the FINAL EXAM? If your situation has strangely taken a left turn, is harder than usual, uncomfortable, and even unrecognizable to some degree, and you've passed the previous tests; then more than likely, it's because you're taking your final exam, for entrance to your next level! It's this test that will lead to promotion or the repetition of coursework. Why did you expect the Final to be like all of the other tests and pop quizzes? The Final is specifically designed to test you in such a way that when you pass it, there's no question about whether or not you're ready for the next level, because you will be.

Today, there are many teachers who advance challenged students to the next grade simply because they do not want to take the time to teach them, nor do they really care. These students get promoted to the next grade level, when clearly they're just not ready, nor equipped to handle everything that comes along with the advancement. In contrast, those of us that are in Christ have the Holy Spirit as our teacher and He makes sure that we have mastered our current level before promoting us to the next. So please, pay close attention to the not-so-always-obvious lessons, study to show yourself approved, and don't get distracted; because all of the smaller tests that you've passed have led up to this moment... your Final Exam! If you were not ready for this test, you wouldn't be going through what you're going through. You've got it because you can handle it, as He never gives us more than we can bear:

No temptation has seized you except what is common to man. And God is faithful; he will not let you be tempted beyond what you can bear. But when you are tempted, he will also provide a way out so that you can stand up under it. 1 Corinthians 10:13

Take the test, pass it, and graduate to your next level. Remember, your teacher will never test you without first equipping you with the answers. The Final Exam is what you've prepared for this entire season. It's the Final that carries the most weight, and regardless of how well you've done up to this point, it's this test that will determine your next level. So yes, you're going through, but it's just a test. You're taking your Final, so pass and prepare for graduation, because it's time for promotion!

God wants you to pass because He wants to promote you... for HIS glory!!!

Joseph had to pass a series of tests before being promoted to second-in-command in all of Egypt; from being thrown into a pit and into Egyptian slavery by his brothers, to pushing off Potiphar's wife with her attempt to seduce him. Yet, in all of this, he never denied the Lord, and still walked upright before Him!

Even after Joseph's promotion, there was yet another exam. We'll call this one the "Post-Final." When Joseph's brothers had to come to Egypt during the famine (the same ones who had thrown him in a pit, leaving him for dead), they had to come to their brother so that they might live. Now, they needed their brother's mercy.

Joseph had the power to shut them down, be revengeful and kill them all; but he did not. Instead, he exercised grace, forgiveness, mercy, and love. As hurt as he was about what his brothers had done to him, he forgave and embraced them. Joseph understood that what they meant for evil, God meant for good.

"But as for you, ye thought evil against me; but God meant it unto good, to bring to pass, as it is this day, to save much people alive." Genesis 50:20 (KJV)

Always remember, that when God elevates you, it's much bigger than you; and when the Lord promotes you, it's because He already knows how you will handle the power that He gives you. He knows that even though you could be revengeful against those who may have previously wronged you, you'll choose His way instead. You'll choose love, forgiveness, grace, mercy, and compassion... just as He did with you.

The reason everyone will not get promoted is because the Lord already knows what's in their hearts; and how they'd handle the blessing, the power, the money, the spouse, the business, etc. Nothing is hidden from Him, and everything lays bare before Him. So, even when we think we're fooling man, God is never fooled.

"Nothing in all creation is hidden from God's sight. Everything is uncovered and laid bare before the eyes of him to whom we must give account." Hebrews 4:13

While man looks at the outward appearance, God looks at the heart. David, a man after God's own heart, said it this way, "Create in me a clean heart, O God; and renew a right spirit within me." (Psalms 51:10 KJV) David understood that he needed the Lord to clean him up in a way that he could never cleanse himself. He understood that the only way to please God was to surrender His whole heart to Him and instead of pretending to be perfect and having it all together, he just presented himself yielded and broken before the Heart Fixer...the Potter...the King of kings...the Great I AM. If promotion seems to be delayed in your life, ask the Lord to search you, and create in you a clean heart; because that's the only kind of heart that will make it to, and through the next level. It's the only kind of heart that He's pleased with.

As we matriculate through the University of Life, we go through a series of testing designed to make us stronger, stretch us, and grow us up in Him. These tests are specifically designed for each student according to their strengths, weaknesses, and purpose. These tests are only given when the student is ready to take them, according to the teacher, the Holy Spirit. So, if taken and not passed, it's not because the student wasn't ready... but rather, because the student did not know they were ready. So, instead of having the ability to identify certain situations as tests, they erroneously viewed it as God forsaking or punishing them, when in fact, it should have been viewed as God's vehicle to promote them:

"For promotion cometh neither from the east, nor from the west, nor from the south. But God is the judge: he putteth down one, and setteth up another."

Psalms 75:6-7 (KJV)

Promotion comes neither from the east nor the west, but from the Lord. Have you ever known anyone to be promoted without showing due cause for the promotion? Who gets promoted to the next level without proving that they've excelled on the current level? We know that God will promote us in the natural based upon what is happening in the spirit. He will reward us openly for what we do in private. Truly, He is a rewarder to them that diligently seek Him. Although having a natural ability to do   something is great, God does not promote based on that, otherwise it wouldn't be a supernatural promotion.

We must be determined to pass our series of tests and Final Exam, so much so, that when trials and adversity come our way, we don't shrink back, but REJOICE! We rejoice because we recognize it as an opportunity to grow into maturity in Christ, as God takes us from faith to faith, and from glory to glory! Hallelujah!!! When we go through our tests and trials, James tells us to "Count It All Joy."

My brethren, count it all joy when ye fall into divers temptations; Knowing this, that the trying of your faith worketh patience. But let patience have

her perfect work, that ye may be perfect and entire,
wanting nothing. James 1:2-4 (KJV)

When the Lord brings you to a test, pop quiz, or final exam; it's because He knows you're equipped to pass! The question is... do you know? Please realize that nothing can happen to you unless the Lord allows it to be so. He is sovereign, and anything that occurs does so within the framework of His sovereignty. This applies to every mountaintop experience, every valley, every test, and every trial. This even applies to the accuser of the brethren; for he can do nothing unless the Lord allows it:

One day the angels came to present themselves
before the LORD, and Satan also came with them.
The LORD said to Satan, "Where have you come
from?"

Satan answered the LORD, "From roaming
through the earth and going back and forth in it."

Then the LORD said to Satan, "Have you consid-
ered my servant Job? There is no one on earth like
him; he is blameless and upright, a man who fears
God and shuns evil." Job 1:6-8

There are even times when God will be silent with us, just to see if we truly trust Him... I mean, REALLY trust Him! He wants us to get to a place like that of the three Hebrew boys: Shadrach, Meshach, and Abednego, where we can say, "We know our God is able to deliver us, but EVEN IF HE DOESN'T, we STILL won't bow down!" Now, as tough as it may have been for these three boys to decline the king's food, and stick with their own diet, they did it anyway; and had enough faith and courage in the One who is above all kings, including Nebuchadnezzar. Their faith was in the King of kings! Now, even though denying the king's food was indeed a significant test, it was not the Final Exam.

The Final Exam consisted of them making a decision to choose death over bowing down to another god; and although they had great certainty and confidence in their God's ability to deliver them, they did not allow the mystery of the outcome to affect their allegiance. Their faith was not that God would do it, but that He could do it; and their minds were made up that..."even if He didn't do it"... they still would not bow down to another god, and would rather be thrown into the fire than to disappoint their first love. This is the level at which we should love the Lord... with all of our heart, with all of our mind, and with all of our soul. Then he said to them all: "If anyone would come after me, he must deny himself and take up his cross daily and follow me." Luke 9:23

To follow Jesus means to follow Him through the good and the bad, through sickness and in health, through sunshine and rain, through heartache and pain... even unto death. The beautiful thing about being a follower of the Lord is that He promises to never leave nor forsake us. He tells us that He will be with us even until the end of the earth. So when we belong to Him, just as He was with the three Hebrew boys in the fiery furnace, so will He be with those who walk according to His way.

Then Nebuchadnezzar the king was astonished, and rose up in haste, and spake, and said unto his counselors, Did not we cast three men bound into the midst of the fire? They answered and said unto the king, True, O king. He answered and said, Lo, I see four men loose, walking in the midst of the fire, and they have no hurt; and the form of the fourth is like the Son of God. Then Nebuchadnezzar came near to the mouth of the burning fiery furnace, and spake, and said, Shadrach, Meshach, and Abednego, ye servants of the Most High God, come forth, and come hither. Then Shadrach, Meshach, and Abednego, came forth of the midst of the fire. And the princes, governors, and captains, and the king's counselors, being gathered together, saw these men, upon whose bodies the fire had no power, nor was an hair of their head singed, neither were their coats changed, nor the smell of fire had passed on them. Daniel 3:24-27 (KJV)

We see men and women of God all throughout God's Word who have had series of tests throughout their lives, followed by final exams for entrance to another level, and then the Final Exam. Abraham took His Final Exam, and was willing to sacrifice His only son; but God provided a ram in the bush. Esther took her Final Exam and said, "If I perish, then let me perish," and was given favor from the King for herself and her people. The three Hebrew boys took their Final Exam, and said that they knew that God was able to deliver them; but even if He didn't, they still would not bow down! As a result, they were accompanied by a fourth man in the fire, Jesus Himself, and exited the fire without a burn, or without smelling like smoke! Finally, our Lord and Savior, Jesus Christ took His Final Exam by hanging on an old rugged cross, for your sins and mine; and when the going got tough, he even asked if this cup could be taken from Him; and then went on to say, "but nevertheless, not my will; but thine will be done!"

The problem is that many say they want Jesus, but they also want to hold on to their lives that He died to deliver them from. Paul said, "For to me, to live is Christ and to die is gain." (Philippians 1:21) Hanging on to dead relationships, old habits, old behaviors, old ways of talking, old ways of walking, and old, dead ways of living will not work. No one can serve two masters... you will love one, and hate the other. Jesus said it this way, "The man who loves his life will lose it, while the man who hates his life in this world will keep it for eternal life." (John 12:25)   He's a Holy God, and will not be attached to a harlot.   He's coming back for a faithful bride; one without spot or wrinkle, and with no other lovers. He will not be coming back for the adulterous bride. He will not be coming back for the double-minded bride, and He won't be returning for the unprepared bride. He's coming back for a beautiful bride... one after His own heart who knows, without a shadow of a doubt, who her first love is. She must be without spot or wrinkle, and she must be ready.

At that time the kingdom of heaven will be like ten virgins who took their lamps and went out to meet the bridegroom. Five of them were foolish and five were wise. The foolish ones took their lamps but did not take any oil with them. The wise, however, took oil in jars along with their lamps. The bridegroom was a long time in coming, and they all became drowsy and fell asleep. At midnight the cry rang out: 'Here's the bridegroom! Come out to meet him! Then all the virgins woke up and trimmed their lamps. The foolish ones said to the wise, 'Give us some of your oil; our lamps are going out. 'No,' they replied, 'there may not be enough for both us and you. Instead, go to those who sell oil and buy some for yourselves. But while they were on their way to buy the oil, the bridegroom arrived. The virgins who were ready went in with him to the wedding banquet. And the door was shut. Later the others also came. 'Sir! Sir!' they said. 'Open the door for us!' But he replied, 'I tell you the truth, I don't know you. There-fore keep watch, because you do not know the day or the hour.

Matthew 25:1-13

Many people are asleep today. They believe that the Lord will accept them in their mess. However, this is not the Word. John the Baptist had a very clear message of repentance, which was used to prepare the way of the Lord for Jesus' first coming. Today, the spirit of Elijah is clear, as it was with John the Baptist. The remnant is crying loud and sparing not to, "prepare ye the way of the Lord" for the rapture of His church, as well as the second coming of Christ. Will you be ready? If not, then today is the day of salvation. He stands at the door of your heart, knocking. Will you let Him in? If you would like to receive salvation right now, simply pray:

Lord Jesus, thank you for loving me. Thank you for dying on the cross for me, shedding your precious blood for me, and taking my place. I believe that you died so that I may have eternal life; and I believe that you were raised from the dead on the third day; and now sit at the right hand of the Father. I also believe that when you went up to be with the Father, you sent us your Holy Spirit, the Comforter, so that we would be empowered to live a life that pleases you; and so that we would never be alone. Please forgive me for all of my sins, by word, by thought and by deed. Please create in me a clean heart and renew a right spirit within me. Please come into my heart, and fill me with your Holy Spirit, with the evidence of speaking in tongues. I want to come into right relationship with you, be born again by your spirit, and have the ability to hear your voice and obey you. I receive my salvation, and baptism of the Holy Spirit. I give you thanks and praise, Lord Jesus. In your name I pray, Amen.

If you sincerely prayed that prayer by faith from your heart, then the angels in heaven are rejoicing. You have been born again by the Spirit of the Living God, and you are now a babe in Christ. Now, just like a baby, you must stay fed and nurtured in order to grow up properly. Be sure to pray, and read God's word daily. As you do this, the Lord will give you what to pray, guide you, and lead you into all truth; because the Holy Spirit is the Spirit of truth. Also, ask the Lord to lead you to a Bible-teaching, Bible-believing, Body of Believers, where you can have regular fellowship with other saints. Finally, because the Lord paid such a high price for you by suffering, bleeding and dying on that old rugged cross... He wants all of you; and because of His love for you, He will not accept less than one hundred percent. Thankfully, the good news is, "what's impossible with man is possible with God." This is why we must die daily to our flesh, and put it under the subjection of God's Word. If we don't kill it, it will eventually kill us. This is why Paul talks about the two natures warring one with another:

We know that the law is spiritual; but I am unspiritual, sold as a slave to sin. I do not understand what I do. For what I want to do I do not do, but what I hate I do. And if I do what I do not want to do, I agree that the law is good. As it is, it is no longer I myself who do it, but it is sin living in me. I know that nothing good lives in me, that is, in my sinful nature. For I have the desire to do what is good, but I cannot carry it out. For what I do is not the good I want to do; no, the evil I do not want to do—this I keep on doing. Now if I do what I do not want to do, it is no longer I who do it, but it is sin living in me that does it. Romans 7:14-20

He's MAKING YOU... And the "HEAT" you're experiencing is necessary for where He's taking you... STAY on the wheel!!!

"**A**nd we know that ALL THINGS work together for good to those who love God, to those who are the called according to His purpose."

Romans 8:28 (NKJV, emphasis mine)

So many of us, when we bake cakes, use pre-made box mix. Yes, we've come to appreciate Duncan Hines® and Betty Crocker®. It's quick and easy and we like it without a whole lot of hassle; but I'm reminded of my grandfather, who was a real chef, and made EVERYTHING from scratch. When I say everything, I mean everything! We had homemade chicken and dumplings, buttermilk biscuits that would melt in your mouth, chicken a la king, fresh greens... and on Fridays, we'd have fried fish with cabbage, and cornbread from scratch. He was even particular about his pancakes. On Saturday mornings, he'd take out his iron griddle... plug it up... wait for it to get searing hot... then mix the batter and begin pouring. He was so meticulous that he'd always throw out the first three pancakes, and to this day, I'm not sure why he did that. I do know that it had something to do with the pancakes not being perfected to his liking. This was due to the fact that the griddle had not yet gotten to its full "heating" capacity. Many times, we'd say, "Da-da," as we'd affectionately call him, "Don't throw those pancakes away... we'll eat them"! But as the experienced chef, he was determined to make sure that the pancakes were right!

So it is with the children of the Most High King. The ingredients that go into a cake represent every aspect and experience of life that makes us who we are...and just like cake batter, you can get a "taste" of what something will become... but it's not until it hits the "heat" that it becomes what it is purposed to be. See, simply having the "ingredients" is one thing, and mixing them all together is another; but until that heat hits it, it will never become all that it is destined and purposed to be! Even so, God knows just the right temperature, and length of time that is necessary to keep us in the fire in order to perfect us according to His perfect will for our lives. So, don't look at Susie, and wonder why she was only in the oven at 250 degrees for a mere 25 minutes! No baby.... Where God is taking you, you're going to need more heat, and more time. He knows exactly what it's going to take to make you!

We're so accustomed to this microwave, "have it your way" society, but the reality is, that's not real life! No! Real life uses a conventional oven. Real life uses heat from fire, not radiation! Real life bakes slowly, to ensure that things are not just done on the outside, but from the inside out! Stay on the wheel, and let Him finish making you!

When we look at David, the Bible tells us that David was anointed as king fifteen years prior to him sitting on the throne! God knew that from the time of David's anointing to appointing, He needed to be "processed."

As the Lord elevates us in Him, and propels us into purpose, we need to understand that some luggage will have to be dropped off, and left behind! Where God is taking you, you can't take that emotional baggage!   Where God is taking you, you've got to leave your affection for that married man behind. Where God is taking you, that anger, bitterness and unforgiveness can't go! Why are you still angry about what someone did to you over 20 years ago? They've moved on, they're happy and haven't thought about you for a very long time; but you're still carrying that hurt, anger, and unforgiveness. Let it go! You can't take it where God is taking you. There's no room for it! For this journey, you'll even be required to leave some people behind. You know who they are; they're usually the ones that pop up first in your mind. Everyone can't go where you're going. Everyone can't go where God is taking you. Everyone is not willing to pay the price, nor is everyone called to accompany you.

The 16 Dating Essentials... and when it's a good idea to "keep it moving..."

There are some basic dating rules for singles that are critical to follow. Many of us have already been through the fire... so you don't have to!

1. If a man's cell phone frequently goes to voicemail for hours at a time (usually on weekends)... and when you do reach him, he has all kinds of excuses as to why he's always too busy to answer his phone for extended periods of time... that's an indication that he's more than likely NOT available, and is probably even married. If you don't know where he lives, and you communicate with him mostly via text messaging, or feel like he has you on some kind of "rotating schedule..." Please don't waste your time... That's not the kind of man you want in your life. Keep it moving!

2. If a man holds a title/position in the church, and when you speak with him, he spews more profanity than most, and/or sexual innuendoes... Keep it moving! (Actually, in this case, keep it moving EVEN IF he doesn't carry a church title!)

3. If a man has burned bridges with ALL of his ex-girlfriends... and isn't cordial with at least two of them... Keep It Moving!

4. Beware of a man who has few, to no male friends that help to keep him accountable. This is usually a sign that he may have an issue submitting to authority.   How he submits to authority and sound counsel is an indication of how He submits to God. Again, Keep It Moving!

5. Beware of a man who makes you wonder what he did before he met you.... because now, he wants to spend ALL of his free time with you... which is   basically smothering!   If you can't breathe, keep it moving! In the beginning, this type of attention may be flattering, however, as time goes

on, you'll see that the root of it is usually a result of deep insecurity, and rejection. In other words, his affection isn't rooted in the right things... this is a brother who needs healing.

6. Beware of a man who collects or watches porn (Women usually pass this off as being normal or harmless just because he's a man), but please know that watching porn is usually an indicator of an unfaithful or sexually discontent man, who has a lust spirit, and thereby, is not ready for a relationship with you. He needs to be delivered. So again... Keep it moving! (Pray for his deliverance though.)

7. If he has multiple children by multiple women, and has never raised any in the same home with him.... AND his present behavior shows NO FRUIT of a changed lifestyle... Keep it moving! He's still growing up!

8. MAJOR ONE: If he's seriously talking marriage within the first 30 days of meeting... don't

just keep it moving... RUN QUICKLY! As serious as marriage is, why would he be so pushy about something so significant in such a short period of time? Put the brakes on... and allow the Lord to show you who he really is.

9. If you don't know exactly where he lives or works, nor do you have a home telephone number for him, he's probably married... so DEFINITELY... Keep it moving!

10. MAJOR ONE FOR CHRISTIAN SINGLES: If he tells you, "God told me that you're my wife," DON'T run to the altar just yet.... But get your OWN confirmation from the Lord... No matter how long it takes... God will let you know if you ask Him! Just TRUST HIM!!!

11. If just about every time you go out, you find yourself reaching in your purse to pay.... Keep it moving! If you've been paying his way for the TWO of you to be entertained, or what have you... then why do you need him? Are you looking for a

liability, or an asset? ? Truly, you are not desperate, nor do you have to buy anyone's time, attention, or affection! Sure, once you're in a relationship, and have determined that this is someone who is worthy of you, and your time, then every now and then, you can treat. However, you are not a doormat, nor were you born yesterday! Recognize the signs early, and respond accordingly. Being treated like a queen does not mean "you treat" the majority of the time you go out...

12. If a man asks you for money within the first 90 days of meeting... Keep it moving! (Because if he's comfortable enough to ask you that soon... he's done it before...and it's regular behavior for him...believe that!) Most men have too much dignity, and respect for themselves to ask a woman, they just met, for money... Now really, WHO does that?

13. If he has never really had to submit to authority.... In other words, was he raised by mostly women, and if so, how does he treat

women...? (and NOT JUST his mother?) Is he in a profession or ministry where he has to submit to male authority? If not, does he have men in his life who make him accountable? Now, I'm NOT talking about the ones who go along with whatever he does, and have no courage to call him to the carpet... when necessary.   If they are not being held accountable   from   a   character   and   integrity standpoint, and have never really had to submit to authority, then you may want to step back so you can focus in on the panoramic view. These types of men usually have issues with pride and humility... so, please, Keep it moving!

14.   BE ON ALERT for occupations that project *excessive* amounts of bravado: i.e., Athletes, Police Officers, etc.   Now, of course this doesn't apply to all men in these professions, but just keep your eyes open if you are dating someone in these kinds of positions... and no matter *what* their position, always watch for *fruit.*

15.   Beware of a man who doesn't respect his own mother, as well as a man whose mother won't let him be a man...and he's ok with that! Mama's boys have difficulty being boys and men at the same time.

16.   Finally... Beware of a man who INDULGES in conspicuous consumption, and simply purchases items with the intent of being noticed! (i.e., 14 homes, 12 brand-new luxury cars) but no one to share these items with.... Now of course, there's nothing wrong with a man having "things," however, if he's the type who lives as though he needs "the things" to make him a man... then that's a problem. Keep it moving... there's usually a lot of drama associates with those types. Not to mention, typically when people behave in that way, it's an attempt to fill a greater emptiness that multiple billions in the bank, and hundreds of cars, houses, etc... STILL couldn't fill.

In ALL things, be prayerful, use wisdom, and allow the Holy Spirit to lead you. In doing so, you will avoid many unnecessary pitfalls! Don't place your pearls before swine.... You deserve so much more!

Major Myths of **CHRIST**ianity

I've decided to add this portion to this work... be-cause at the end of the day, this is not about me, but about sharing the love of Jesus Christ with others, and being a witness for Him. In addition, without FIRST knowing HIM, yet hoping for or pursuing a relationship with the opposite sex, is certainly putting the cart before the horse. When we put Him first, HE adds all of the other things to us. (see Matthew 6:33) However, we must keep things in proper prospective. Therefore, in Major Myths of CHRISTianity, I share my story of how I came to know the Lord; along with many fallacies that are widely believed by many, as it pertains to this walk of discipleship. ~Shea A. Cameron

Myth # 1: "I plan to give my life to the Lord, but I have to GET MYSELF TOGETHER FIRST!" This is one of the BIGGEST lies straight from the pit of hell!   Don't you know that you will NEVER get yourself together without the Lord?!? Please, don't worry about trying to clean yourself up or get right first; just come as you are. Let HIM clean you up... Let HIM give you a new, clean, heart of flesh.... Let HIM do the work, because you are not able to do it on your own.   Just trust Him, as He says, "...the day you hear His voice... harden NOT your heart!" Trust Him... I am a WITNESS. If He did it for me, then HE can and will do it for you! Just trust Him! (Roman 10:9-10) Even after He first saved me, I STILL struggled with smoking cigarettes, but WANTED to quit. I would buy a pack, smoke two or three, throw it away.... Buy another pack, smoke two or three... get so convicted, and throw it away. This cycle continued for a few months UNTIL one day, He spoke to me. I was sitting in my car, at a stop light... and He said, "ASK ME TO TAKE AWAY THE DESIRE!" My God!!! I prayed that prayer, and was INSTANTLY delivered from cigarettes.   From this, the Lord taught me that we only struggle with what we DESIRE. However, if we don't desire it, it's not a struggle! What wrong desires do you need for Him to remove from you today?

Myth #2: You can live ANY kind of way, and STILL make it in. NO!!! The Word of God declares, "Enter through the narrow gate. For wide is the gate and broad is the road that leads to destruction, and many enter through it. But small is the gate and narrow the road that leads to life and only a few find it." Matthew 7:13-14

"Do you not know that the wicked will not inherit the kingdom of God? Do not be deceived: Neither the sexually immoral, nor idolaters, nor adulterers, nor male prostitutes, nor homosexual offenders, nor thieves, nor the greedy, nor drunkards, nor slanderers, nor swindlers will inherit the kingdom of God. And that is what some of you WERE. (Past tense) But you were washed, you were sanctified, you were justified in the name of the Lord Jesus Christ and by the Spirit of our God. 1 Corinthians 6:9-11 (Words in parentheses are my own, to emphasize the meaning of the text.)

Please know that GOD IS NOT MOCKED! He requires Holiness! HE requires His offering HIS WAY..."but on Cain and his offering he did not look with favor. So Cain was very angry, and his face was downcast. Then the Lord said to Cain, "Why are you angry? Why is your face downcast? If you do what is right, will you not be accepted? But if you do not do what is right, sin is crouching at your door; it desires to have you, but you must master it." Genesis 4:5-7

He will HELP YOU to live a life that pleases Him, IF this is your desire. JUST RESPOND to His rebuke and correction! This is why Jesus sent us the Holy Ghost! HE IS OUR HELPER!!! Remember, Jesus did NOT leave us comfortless, or helpless!

My son, if you accept my words and store up my commands within you, TURNING YOUR EAR TO WISDOM and applying your heart to understanding, and if you call out for insight and cry aloud for under-standing, and if you look for it as for silver

and search for it as for hidden treasure, then you will understand the fear of the Lord and find the knowledge of God. For the Lord gives wisdom, and from his mouth come knowledge and understanding.
Proverbs 2:1-6 (emphasis mine)

Myth #3: You have to be in a church building in order for God to save you, and be born again. NOT!!! When the Lord saved and converted me in December of 1994, I was in my house, by myself, smoking weed and drinking wine. This is what I would do when I came home from work to "unwind." On this particular night, I felt a demonic presence. I knew it wasn't what some would call "tripping" off of the weed, but the presence was so strong that I could feel the evil. I was very afraid, because I had enough sense to know that "whatever" this thing was, it was coming for me. Now, at this time, I was just 21 years old, and although I grew up in the church, the church was not in me. I was lost. I was on my way to hell. However, if I didn't know how to do anything else, I knew to get on my knees; and all I remember saying was, "Lord Jesus, please come into my heart." The next thing I know... IMMEDIATELY, I was no longer high, the evil presence had left, and I began to hear the voice of the Lord for the first time in my life. The very first two things that He said to me were to throw away all of my CD's (secular music) and give away all of my clothes. At that time, I would steal clothes out of Saks, Neiman's, Nordstrom's, etc., so I had a closet full of VERY expensive clothing that I had not paid for. Of course the Lord knew about it. This was the beginning of my journey. If you never LONG FOR anything else out of this life; LONG TO HEAR HIS VOICE. It is the most beautiful sound that you will EVER hear as HE says, "MY SHEEP hear my voice." Glory to God!!!

Myth #4: Everyone sitting in the house of God with a title is called by God, and belongs to Him. NOT!!! Jesus was CLEAR on, "BY THEIR FRUIT," NOT their title, will you know them!!! So, if you have so-called leaders who look NOTHING LIKE, ACT NOTHING LIKE, LIVE NOTHING LIKE CHRIST.... More than likely, they are NOT His! If you are in a church that is under this kind of leadership; SEEK THE LORD about WHERE He would have you to be. HE will lead you. Remember," The steps of a good man are ordered by the Lord." Psalm 37:23a (NKJV)

Myth #5: There is such a thing as, "Once saved, always saved." ABSOLUTELY NOT!!! The Word of God declares that we are to "WORK OUT" our soul's salvation with fear and trembling! "... work out your own salvation with fear and trembling; for it is God who works in you both to will and to do for His good pleasure." Philippians 2:12b-13 (NKJV)

Furthermore, if this fallacy were true, then HOW would there be a "great falling away?" (2 Thessalonians 2:3) What would people "fall away" from? Or, HOW would there be "backsliders"? Where would people slide back from??? We are to DIE DAILY to our flesh, and place it under the subjection of the Word of God!!!

Myth #6: HOLINESS equals wearing long skirts, no make-up, and looking matronly. NO! Any devil can wear a long skirt. It's the condition of the HEART that determines how holy a person is. It's NOT what goes into a man that defiles him, but what comes out of Him! For example, when I first got saved, I used to wear red lipstick. However, the Holy Spirit spoke to me one day, and told me not to wear red lipstick. Now, He never told me to not wear make-up; He just said not to wear red lipstick. There must have been something about that red lipstick on my lips that He wasn't pleased with, nor would it glorify Him; so I obeyed. Furthermore, some people believe that women should not wear pants. As for me, the Holy Ghost NEVER convicted me about wearing pants. However, RELIGION will force "blanket rules" on people, without allowing the Holy Ghost to do the work that He was sent to do. Ask the Lord to re-mold you, and re-shape you in HIS image. He will do it, gently and lovingly, by His Spirit. He's SO good like that! Just make sure that you YIELD and SURRENDER when HE tells you what to do, as WHATEVER HE TELLS YOU, will

ALWAYS be for your OWN GOOD... and for HIS GLORY! TRUST AND OBEY HIM!

Myth #7: Since God is a God of "LOVE," He will never allow a man to go to hell. NO!!! Don't believe the hype! Although hell was created for the devil and his angels; man sends himself there when He REJECTS what Jesus did for him at Calvary. HOW does HE reject it? By NOT believing, and by DISOBEYING the Word of God! The wages of sin is death, but the gift of God is eternal life through Christ Jesus our Lord. You cannot live a raggedy life without TRULY repenting from your heart, and expect to make it in. The Word of God even declares that the righteous will SCARCELY be saved... HOW MUCH MORE the ungodly and the sinner?!?! (1 Peter 4:18) Choose ye THIS DAY whom you will serve!!! Tomorrow is not promised!!!

Myth #8: "I know that I am a good person. I have not murdered anyone. People like me, so I know I will go to heaven." NO, you will NOT!!! Not without the Blood of Jesus on your life!!! The Word of God declares that, "our righteousness is as filthy rags before the Lord." (Isaiah 64:6) We were born into sin, and shaped in iniquity... which is why we MUST BE BORN AGAIN!!!!! (John 3:3-8) The blood of JESUS is the ONLY THING that will wash away sin... NOT GOOD WORKS! Are you covered in His blood?!?

Myth #9: If I am credentialed, have attended seminary, and am well-versed in scripture, then I am ok with the Lord. NOT!!! Judas was a scholar as well, but lifted his eyes up in hell. If you NEVER learn Hebrew, you MUST be BORN AGAIN!!! If you NEVER exegete the Greek, you STILL MUST be BORN AGAIN!!! The ONLY WAY to TRULY worship the Lord is in SPIRIT AND IN TRUTH!!! TRUE WORSHIPPERS have been born again by HIS SPIRIT!!! Paul asked, "Have you RECEIEVED SINCE YOU BELIEVED?!?!" (Acts 19:2, punctuation is mine.) You MUST be BORN AGAIN!!!

Myth #10: EVERYONE is a child of God! NOT!!!! Jesus once said to the religious leaders of His day,

"You belong to your father, the devil, and you want to carry out your father's desire. He was a murderer from the beginning, not holding to the truth, for there is no truth in him. When he lies, he speaks his native language, for he is a liar and the father of lies." (John 8:44) Remember, BY THEIR FRUIT YOU WILL KNOW THEM! This is why it's SO important to be as WISE as serpents, but as HARMLESS as doves. ASK THE LORD to give you wisdom, understanding, and discernment so that you will be able to SEE with HIS EYES, HEAR with HIS EARS, and THINK with HIS MIND! This is why the Word of God declares that, we have to"... LET THIS MIND (the mind of Christ) be in us that was also in Christ Jesus!" (Philippians 2:5)

FINAL MYTH: Being saved is a hard concept for me. This whole talk of "Kingdom" is nothing more than a religious fad. NOT!!!!! Jesus was VERY CLEAR! HE said, "SEEK YE FIRST, the Kingdom of God, and HIS Righteousness, and ALL OF THESE THINGS will be added unto you!!! (Matthew 6:33

KJV emphasis mine) The first step is to acknowledge that you are a sinner in need of a Savior. That Savior is Jesus Christ. HE is the King of kings and the Lord of lords. Ask Him to forgive you for all of your sins, to come live in your heart, and to fill you with His Holy Spirit. The Word of God declares,

"If you then, though you are evil, know how to give good gifts to your children, how much more will your Father in heaven give the Holy Spirit to those who ask him?" Luke 11:13

JUST ASK! Ask Him to forgive you for your sins. ASK HIM to come into your heart. ASK HIM for His Holy Ghost. Also, when you ASK, ASK IN FAITH; for WITHOUT FAITH IT IS IMPOSSIBLE TO PLEASE HIM! He that cometh to God MUST BELIEVE that HE IS... and that HE IS A REWARDER OF THEM THAT DILIGENTLY SEEK HIM! (Hebrews 11:6 KJV, emphasis mine)

That if you confess with your mouth, "Jesus is Lord", and believe in your heart that God raised him from the dead, you will be saved. For it is with your heart that you believe and are justified, and it is with your mouth that you confess and are saved. As the Scripture says, "Anyone who trusts in him will never be put to shame." Romans 10:9-11

Will you BELIEVE, REPENT, and RECEIVE TODAY??? TODAY is the day of SALVATION!!!

"For the Son of Man came to seek and to save what was lost." Luke 19:10

Conclusion

Once we are presented with the truth about something, we then have the option of making a deliberate decision to either take heed to its instruction, or ignore it as if we have heard nothing at all.

Now having read the pages of NO FREE MILK, how will you choose? Will you embrace all that God has ordained for you and trust that His way is far greater than your present experience? Maybe you are afraid that if you release the chains of the past that you will lose the comfort of convenience, although compromised.

I want you to know with certainty that, "The blessing of the Lord, it maketh rich, and he addeth no sorrow to it." (Proverbs 10:22, KJV) Yes, when we acknowledge the Lord, surrender our life and will, and seek His wisdom and instruction, it results in blessings without drama, mess, or emotional casualty.

The challenge for us is to BELIEVE and RECEIVE in confidence the promises of our God. First and foremost, we must be reconciled to God, through Jesus Christ; giving priority to our Creator, and making certain that we don't desperately place our desire to be loved ahead of Him.

The Father is not ONLY concerned with the saving of our spirit, but as the scripture declares, "His divine power has given us everything we need for life and godliness through our knowledge of Him who called us by His own glory and goodness." (2 Peter 1:3)

The objective of NO FREE MILK has been to bring forth healing and wholeness, so that we no longer forfeit our place of sovereign peace in lieu of the temporal, compromising pleasure caused by our brokenness.

Receive the balm of the Father's love my sisters and in doing so, let Him wipe away your tears, alleviate your pain, and produce a new depth of joy from within your soul. Jesus has paid the price for our redemption and reconciliation entirely and even the blessing of a God-fearing husband is for you, according to His will and your desire.

I love you all and THANK YOU for allowing NO FREE MILK to be a purposeful resource, guiding you along the path of destiny ordained for abundant living!